PENTANA PRESS

Take the Reins! – How a Little Horse Sense Can Help You Raise Confident, Responsible Children

Published in the United States by Pentana Press
ISBN 978-0999243909

Printed by CreateSpace a DBA of On-Demand Publishing, LLC

TAKE THE REINS!

How a Little Horse Sense Can Help You Raise Confident, Responsible Children

Kris Lawson's *Take the Reins!, How a Little Horse Sense Can Help You Raise Confident, Responsible Children* (Pentana Press, 2017) interweaves lessons from the arena, early childhood development specialists, and the author's personal study, experience, and passion for children to create a wonderfully pragmatic, no-nonsense approach to raising children. Lawson provides numerous exercises, enough to fill any parenting workshop, while providing wise and thought-provoking tips and quotes that are on target. A parent would be hard pressed *not* to learn a good deal from this book, a book that is on one hand an easy read and on the other a book that one must frequently pause to consider, reflect upon, and strive to implement. This book should help many a parent to *Take the Reins* over their parenting, adding new skills and thoughtfulness into raising children.

Robert Horon, Ph.D., Clinical Psychologist

Take the Reins!...A comprehensive hands-on strategy for parenting! Practical advice with relatable examples and practical exercises for sharpening and applying your skills. Whether a 1000 pound mare or a surly three year old, these techniques work! The bottom line...learn to take the lead in setting clear and consistent expectations as you ride through everyday life.

Melinda Gardner, Grandmother and Mother

An awesome read for every parent, teacher, caring adult or horse owner! From beginning to end Ms. Lawson provides the reality of raising children in a broad spectrum of communities and family dynamics. She supports the reader with thoughtful and meaningful exercises that will help prepare them for challenges as well as examples of positive effective communication.

As a school counselor and public school administrator, I encourage all staff to read *Take the Reins!*. The information is presented in a way that can be used in all settings i.e., home, school, community and not just adult to child but adult to adult.

Take the Reins! is a valuable resource that should be well read and on every bookshelf. It can be used as a book study, parenting program, or for the parent that wants to have the guidance and support to raise a well-rounded caring individual.

Susan M. Kerhoulas
MS Educational Counseling
Public School Administrator, Retired

About the Author

Working her way through college as an instructional aide in a state run childcare center, Kris achieved her goal of becoming a preschool teacher. She taught in a variety of settings, from private and school district run preschools, to the federal Head Start (HS) and Early Head Start (EHS) programs for low income families. After twenty plus years of continuing education and teaching, she became an education specialist and then director in a large inner city EHS and HS program. During her forty year career, Kris was privileged to learn and instruct both teaching staff and parents in the most current research-based theories of positive adult-child interactions, in hundreds of classrooms and family homes. These rich and intimate experiences, along with raising two sons of her own, provided an authentic, real world perspective on which parenting techniques worked and which didn't.

During the past ten years Kris learned everything she possibly could about natural horsemanship from both the "horse-whisperers" and from the horses themselves. The unexpected, but happy marriage of teaching and horsemanship revealed the principles of adult-child interaction that Kris had observed missing in parenting and parenting education. *Take the Reins! How a Little Horse Sense Can Help You Raise Confident, Responsible Children* was the resulting love child!

Kris's retirement careers as a PATH Int. certified Therapeutic Riding Instructor and Equine Specialist in Mental Health and Learning along with teaching parenting through coaching and parenting workshops allows her to continue to learn and to share this relevant and practical knowledge with parents.

Find more information at: parentingwithhorsesense.com and facebook.com/parentingwithhorsesense

TAKE THE REINS!

**How a Little Horse Sense Can Help You
Raise Confident, Responsible Children**

CONTENTS

REFERENCES

"There is no single effort more radical in its potential for saving the world than a transformation of the way we raise our children."

-Marianne Williamson

FOREWORD

Kids + Horses = Great Parenting?

Want great kids? Want to achieve that elusive balance between tough and tender? The Horse-whisperers can guide you in turning challenging behaviors into opportunities to build connection, confidence and self-control!

Who would have thought a forty year veteran of teaching, parenting, and teaching parenting would come to believe that the secret to raising confident, responsible, happy children with grit, and *avoid* raising defiant, entitled, megalomaniacs or helpless, perpetual victims, was **horse sense**? This is how that improbable, but enlightening connection came to be...

There was a nagging sense that I really should be concerned about our neighbor's possible irritation with the music and raucous laughter escaping through the screen door, but when four old girlfriends who hadn't seen each other in years, combine another round of Cosmos with another round of cards, rowdiness rules and judgment recedes. Since no male stripper was magically appearing, we settled on each of us creating a "bucket list" to add to the evening's entertainment. At the top of my short list was horseback riding lessons. Less fermented judgment might have warned me off such an ambitious prospect for a fifty-four year old woman, but sometimes a little liquid courage is just the thing to nudge an aging body out of its comfort zone. This seemingly random event would become a significant contributing factor in clarifying and re-framing my hard earned views on child rearing.

My forty year career that started with teaching preschool, then as an administrator in the federal Head Start and Early Head Start preschool and social service programs allowed me to work with children, parents and teachers in hundreds of classrooms and family homes. Since Head Start holds the highest quality of services for families at its core, I was afforded the opportunity to learn and then train teachers and parents to implement the most current and effective child discipline theories, research and approaches in this very practical and very real environment.

Though I'd worked with families from all walks of life, the Head Start experience brought me into the trenches of working with inner city families with very young children in some extremely rough, high risk situations. I witnessed the worst of what society must consider parenting, as well as amazing love and resilience in the face of extreme life situations. Within that rich and varied context, I learned what worked and what didn't.

As you can imagine, during this work I saw a wide range of parenting styles from wealthy over-protective hovercraft, to drug addicted parents who were in and out of prison. I saw parents who embraced the "my way or the highway," or the detached, "the kids will raise themselves" approach, as well as responsive, connected and strong parents. I worked with parents as young as thirteen and grandparents raising their grandchildren. While observing and supporting these families, I felt that a certain type of misbehavior was on the increase in spite of a plethora of available parenting advice. Do any of the following incidents sound familiar?

As I was absent mindedly perusing the jeans rack at Marshalls, my startled jump was accompanied by an undignified squawk as the hangers slid apart to reveal a pair of sparkling brown eyes above a mischievous smile! Next, I heard a frustrated growl, "Zeke, for the hundredth time, get over here right now or I'm gonna whop your butt!"

In the grocery store, three year old Primrose jumps up and down in the cart like it was a trampoline and shrieks with increasing volume for her favorite treat when her exasperated mom *finally* puts it in the cart. (I'm the ol' girl behind her in line stuffing her clenched fist down her throat to keep from asking, "Do you *enjoy* that ear piercing whine; because you just taught her to do more of it!")

Then, there's seventeen-year-old Orville, driving while texting and crashing "his" new Camaro that daddy bought...for the third time. Eh...Dad's insurance will cover it.

How about little Leon who gets in trouble at middle school for punching another child *again* and it is, of course, the fault of: the other child, the principal, the teacher, the yard supervisor, the misalignment of planets, anyone or anything but Leon! And his parents are right there supporting this delusion.

I overheard a frustrated grandmother at the ranch one day venting, "I've lived this long without being hit or told what to do by a three year old, and I'm not about to start now!" As if it wasn't easy enough to see evidence of an increase in entitled and obnoxious behaviors during a trip to the mall, there are even successful reality television shows about it!

These behaviors are perceived by some parents as minor irritations or just an example of "kids will be kids." Cletus impatiently attempts to get mom's attention with a solid kick to her shin and gets an, "Owww - stop that!" for his trouble. Mom then absent-mindedly returns to her friend on the phone and shares, "Cletus is becoming such a good little soccer player."

Blaming the child or unfortunate genetics is just another all too convenient excuse; "He's such a rotten kid - he takes after his father!" and with that said, *that* parent is relieved of all responsibility. Some parents are at their wits end or are afraid of doing the wrong thing, so do nothing, hoping the situation will improve with time. All of those parents are putting the blinders on to the cumulative negative effects of their child's behavior and their responsibility in creating it.

Experience has shown me that this is just a "tip of the iceberg" peek at the heartbreak and misery in store if those parents continue to ignore the behavior, blame the child or cross their fingers and just hope they'll grow out of it. Unless they pick up the reins and choose a different path, the negative behaviors will increase and become cemented into ugly patterns that are harder to change and have more serious long term consequences the longer they exist. The heartbreak lies in the fact that those are just normal kids, unintentionally being taught some seriously negative lessons and missing the opportunity to learn some powerfully positive ones. These unintentional lessons will impact their ultimate character as well as the quality of rest of their lives.

In the early years of teaching, I became a mom myself. I struggled with all the usual challenges involved in raising two sons while working and added the ridiculous self-induced stress that I should be the perfect parent because, well – I have a degree! Not so much. If there was a mistake to be made, I'm sure I made it. Like most parents, I parented as I was parented and my childhood, as I believe it is for most people, was a mixed bag of wonderful (early years of hand sewn dresses from my doting and creative mom, a funny and brilliant father) and horrendous (the loving father who became a mean alcoholic and a mother absorbed in her own survival). I knew early in my college career that I had to learn a better way if I were ever to be a mom myself, so Child Development became my major and my passion.

So, there I was, a new parent armed to the teeth with book learning, falling back into the learned negative aspects of my parenting more often than I care to admit. The combined experience of parenting my own children and supporting others in their parenting taught me humility and empathy; that most parents are doing the best they can, and that kids are resilient. I learned that in order to mature with true self-esteem and good character, children need a parent who is secure and confident in their own personhood and parenthood. However, my experience and education did not provide adequate answers for how to make that happen for myself or for those I was trying to help.

Now, in semi-retirement, I've stepped back and taken a more experienced perspective on dealing with "problem children." Observing the steady increase in those obnoxious behaviors convinced me that there was something missing from parent-child relationships today, something which was evident in a more normal, accepted way in previous generations and which still exists in cultures that are either less impacted by modern society or that have intentionally held on to tenets of the past. I realized that a lack of clear, simple parenting principles that support a *strong, yet loving* parent-child relationship are what was missing. Where I found those principles most clearly defined took me by surprise and became the inspiration for this book.

Those alcohol inspired riding lessons added fuel to the fire of my lifetime obsession with horses. After a few years of leasing a sweet old grey Arabian named Eli and absorbing knowledge about horsemanship like my body happily absorbs calories, circumstances finally allowed the purchase of my very own horse. She was a beautiful, six year old, full of piss and vinegar mare, named Hannah Pentana.

My fantasy horse/woman relationship had the two of us galloping off into the sunset, mane and hair flowing, living happily ever after! Reality smacked me upside the head pretty quickly, and literally when, thanks to a horse-eating cotton tail bunny hopping across our path, I found myself airborne, then planted firmly in the gravel, blurred vision taking in Hannah's swishing tail as she trotted back down the road to the barn. I'm sure if she had digits instead of hooves, she would have found a use for the middle one. Hannah

continued to define for me what horse folks call "mare-ish" (picture headstrong, hormonal teenage girl with attitude).

Hannah's a bit big (16 hands), moody, and instinctively set on establishing herself as the lead mare in our little herd of two. She's a bright girl, as horses go, and she continually reminded me that she could be quite inspired in testing my worthiness as herd leader. She offered a little buck, a kick, a bite, some head tossing, spooking, suddenly stopping and backing up... I'm sure I've yet to see the extent of her creativity! Without Hannah's antics however, I would not have made the amazingly relevant connection between horse sense and parenting.

My first order of business was to build a strong, "person as herd leader," relationship with this horse. I had to wrap my head around the idea that this was going to take a commitment to continuous learning and *work* on my part. Just as with raising children, it was not going to magically happen just because I "*loved horses*" and now I had one of my very own. Horse ownership would prove to be an inspirational process requiring self-awareness, Hannah-awareness and determination if I were to survive with all my parts intact and achieve my dream of connection.

After five years of patience, firmness, and persistence, under the eternally patient, firm, and persistent guidance of Anita Markiewicz, horse woman extraordinaire and my riding instructor, Hannah's "tests" became much fewer and shorter lived. And surprisingly (to me, not to Anita), Hannah

> **Her behavior improved when she was convinced I was on her side, I won't go away, and *I'm capable of being the strong, consistent leader she needs.***

became a much more contented and cooperative horse.

I also came to understand that horses perceive more about us than we do about ourselves. Hannah highlighted my shortcomings as a leader with uncanny precision and clarity. My challenge was accepting that I needed to listen to a horse as a teacher and be open to learning from her. Five years later our relationship has evolved into more than what I could have dreamed of. She has taught me so much! Because it is the nature of horses in general and the temperament of Hannah in particular to continually measure leadership, she will always test me in some way. It's OK. I've learned to recognize her testing behavior on a small scale and to consistently respond in a way that improves our relationship as well as her behavior.

It took time for this skeptical novice to believe Anita when she'd tell me that Hannah's behavior would improve when she was convinced I was on her side, I won't go away, and *I'm capable of being the strong, consistent leader she needs*. There were times I wanted to give up, fearing she was just too much horse for me. But, at the risk of sounding way too new age mystical, Hannah taught me just what I needed to learn at that time in my life.

During those riding and horsemanship lessons, Anita patiently repeated directives (only occasionally raising an eyebrow at the old lady with the crappy memory and no experience) such as, "You've got to be a stronger leader! She'll keep testing you until she knows you are the leader in your little herd of two," "Don't get angry if she makes a mistake, this is your chance to teach her. She needs your support!" And my all-time favorite, "She's looking for limits. She wants freedom within those limits, but she has to know where you draw the line!" I often found myself saying to Anita, *"You should be teaching parenting classes!"*

When the same thoughts kept popping into my brain as I read works by horsemen Mark Rashid, Tom Dorrance, and others and attended clinics by Buck Brannaman, Julie Goodnight and Richard Winters, I finally sensed the glow of a 1000 watt light bulb that had been right in front of me for years! I realized after a lifetime of working with children and families, my own parenting experience and the trials of Hannah that classical horsemanship, old-fashioned horse sense, perfectly described those overarching principles that I saw missing as I witnessed parents searching for answers to today's increasingly challenging parenting issues.

As we pick up the reins and explore this trail together, please know I am a child development specialist, parenting coach, riding instructor and equine specialist. I am *not* a therapist or psychiatrist. The principles offered here are the result of my years of learning and experience, are my opinion, and should not be considered psychological or therapeutic advice. If you have concerns about the health of your relationship with your child, please consult a medical and/or psychological professional.

CHAPTER 1

WHY HORSE SENSE? I'M NOT A "HORSE PERSON!"

Advice from the Experts

As the concerned mom shared the story of her son's stomachache with her doctor (Dr. Leonard Sax, MD, PhD, author of *The Collapse of Parenting; How We Hurt Our Kids When We Treat Them Like Grown-Ups*), the boy looked up from the game on his iPhone to say, "Shut up, mom, you don't know what you're talking about." Dr. Sax says these types of interactions have become more and more common in his practice. He argues that rising levels of obesity, depression, and anxiety among young people, as well as the explosion in prescribing psychiatric medications to kids, can all be traced to parents letting their kids call the shots. Dr. Sax believes parents today have abdicated their authority to their children, profoundly changing our culture in a short period of time in ways that have really harmed kids.

Consider the following advice from some other experts:

- ♡ "Rules without relationship = rebellion."
- ♡ "Your child needs and wants you to be the benevolent leader; the captain of the ship. Children are most comfortable and happy when there is a true leader to keep order, offer guidance and keep them safe."
- ♡ "You don't want to instill fear in your child, but you do want the highest degree of respect. If your child doesn't respect you, then forget about your child liking you."
- ♡ "No matter what you are doing or saying – or not doing or saying, your child is learning something from you or about you. Children's behavior will become consistent with what you are consistently teaching them."
- ♡ "If every time a question is asked, you give the answer, the child doesn't learn to seek the answer on his own."
- ♡ "Discipline isn't a dirty word. It's the precursor to good behavior, and it never comes from bad behavior. People who associate discipline with punishment are wrong; with discipline, punishment is unnecessary. Discipline is a system of learning."
- ♡ "If you are going to teach a child something and have a good relationship, you don't make him learn it – you let him learn it."

These statements of insightful parenting advice aren't quotes from other child development experts such as Drs. Spock, Brazelton, Sears, Piaget, Freud, Erickson, Ginott or Vygotski.

They are from Buck Brannaman, Julie Goodnight, Mark Rashid, Pat Parelli, Ray Hunt, Richard Winters, Tom Dorrance, and other natural horsemanship *horse* trainers and clinicians. Reread the previous quotes and replace the word "child" or "children" with "horse" and you will be reading the original words.

"Natural Horsemanship" addresses what I see as those missing core parenting principles; strong leadership, connection, consistency, self-discipline and partnership, in language that is logical and clear. If we can open our minds to learning from an unexpected source, the horse-whisperers have remarkably relevant wisdom to offer parents who are motivated to raise competent, responsible, loving and happy children.

"Natural Horsemanship"

Over the last few decades there has been a return to more thoughtful and humane methods of horse training based on the psychology of the horse. This approach is a move away from the recent past where more dominating, controlling and in-timidating methods were used. There is a practical reason for this shift – *it works!* A horse's potential to develop a trusting connection with a human while building a pattern of finding comfort in doing the right thing is maximized. This method of interacting with horses, commonly referred to as "natural

horsemanship," is based on training principles that promote positive discipline and trusting, respectful, authoritative relationships.

In working with horses, the effectiveness of the principles of teaching and learning is magnified by the relative danger that comes with their size and ability to harm us. To be successful in working with horses and keep your head attached to your shoulders, one *must* be a confident leader, assured in what he or she wants the horse to do, clear and fair in how it is asked and consistent in the asking. If any of these components are not present, a dangerous 1000 pound monster can be created!

As my journey into the mysteries of horsemanship progressed, five general principles of interaction gradually revealed themselves as critical components for any parent wanting to raise strong, caring, competent adult people. I call them the **Five Mighty C's**. I firmly believe in the power of these principles to prevent children from becoming fifty pound monsters that are even more dangerous than horses because they come with the power of speech and ability to reason!

When referring to riding, the term "natural horsemanship" is a bit of a chuckle - there is really nothing about riding a horse that is particularly "natural" for the horse. We strap a dead cow hide on his back and climb aboard in the very place on his body where a mountain lion would attack – his only blind spot. Then we say, "Now, ignore your five million years of survival instinct and don't be afraid; I've got this. Just carry me wherever I want to go and do exactly as I say!" No problem.

The Five Mighty C's, The Heart of Parenting

The core value of *Take the Reins!*, confident leadership, is woven throughout the Five Mighty C's. You'll also see that each "C" is interconnected, dependent on and supportive of the others. The following is a brief overview of *Take the Reins'!* five principles of parenting, based in natural horsemanship, that are the heart of all adult-child interactions:

1. **Consider** – 1) Your child, 2) yourself and your approach, and 3) your goals and intent.

2. **Connect** – To build the relationship and to open the door to communication. Actively listen and connect to the logical, thinking side of your child's brain before attempting to reason.

3. **Communicate** – Listen more. Be mindful and in control of your emotions. Acknowledge the *try* and communicate clearly. Become a "*Kidwhisperer.*"

4. **Co-operate** - *We* create "*win-win*" solutions. Use collaboration to develop self-control, positive decision making and responsibility. Build acceptable solutions together.

5. **Consistency** – You are *always* teaching. Model and enforce expectations and consequences across all situations and circumstances. Have a plan.

> Use these 3 principles during "teachable moments."

The order of the principles is purposeful:

♡ Working through the three steps of the first principle, **Consider,** is critical before you implement the three action steps, which are:

♡ **Connect, Communicate, Co-operate** - *in that order,* during a teachable moment.

♡ When you are practicing the middle three C's, and you have established family values and rules, you must be **Consistent** in upholding them.

The five principles are explained in depth and practice exercises are offered for each of the **Five Mighty C's** in Chapters 3, 4, 5, 6, and 7, respectively. Chapter 8 will explore the challenges and benefits of choosing and maintaining change.

When you implement the pattern created using the middle three C's, **Connect, Communicate and Co-operate**, during behavioral challenges, your children will learn character building and life enhancing lessons that include but are not limited to:

♡ You are a safe haven for sharing and understanding emotions and will help him/her regain emotional control.

♡ Empathy and the ability to take another's perspective.

♡ Acceptable ways to express negative emotions.

♡ Impulse control and delayed gratification.

♡ Behaviors and choices have consequences.

♡ How to make decisions and solve problems.

♡ Conflicts can end in win-win solutions.

Incorporate all five of the Mighty C's into your parenting and the results can be dynamic and life changing! You'll interact with your infants, young children, school-age, and teenage children in ways that encourage optimal brain development, connection, creative thinking, responsibility, resilience and positive, independent problem solving. You will *avoid* raising children who treat you, relatives, teachers and others to an attitude of entitlement, who expect someone else to make decisions or solve problems for them, who cannot accept responsibility or learn from mistakes, who cannot constructively deal with their own or other's emotions, or show compassion.

Try to identify any parallels with your experience as a parent as you read the following brief example of the Five Mighty C's in action in the horse world.

Adorable 120 pound Katie wants to get her 1600 pound draft horse with attitude, Big Mamma, into the horse trailer. If Big Mamma don't want to go, Mamma don't go! Unfortunately, experience has taught Big Mamma that all she has to do is intimidate Katie and Katie will get fearful and give up. Katie's weak leadership has unintentionally but effectively taught Mamma to ignore her and Big Mamma has successfully trained Katie to back off.

> *"You can get a horse to do something if you're tough enough, just like you can with a human. But a willing communication is a different matter."*

An old time, "Oh, *I'll* get her in," wrangler might use ropes and a whip to force Mamma in. But what will happen the next time Big Mamma is asked to get in the trailer? Would the *real* lessons from this type of encounter build a long term positive relationship and willing cooperation?

Katie had just attended a natural horsemanship clinic so it was a new day for Big Mamma. First, Katie considered her goal – use the challenge of getting Big

Mamma into the trailer to establish a positive, "human as herd leader" relationship. Then she considered what motivates Mamma and gets her connected to her thinking brain, which is primarily laziness and comfort sprinkled with food. (I do not recommend using food as a reward with children.) Katie made a plan.

Katie chose a time when she didn't need to hurry, to re-introduce Big Mamma to the trailer. She trotted her in a circle on a lead line when away from the trailer, allowing her to rest only when she was close to it, making the right thing easy and the wrong thing difficult. After a few minutes, Mamma stepped her dinner plate sized front feet up inside the trailer, then her entire dainty self, and was allowed to rest and munch a bit of hay. Another few minutes of this routine and Big Mamma decided that the trailer might just be an okay place to be. When she willingly stepped up and in and stood quietly for a few minutes, Katie took her back to her stall to rest and to eat.

A couple of days later Katie repeated the process and in less than five minutes Momma was comfortably standing inside the trailer munching from her hay bag. Katie closed her in, drove around for a bit, returned and let her out to go eat. On Saturday, when Katie needed Mamma to load so they could attend a

> **A strong, connected relationship and cooperation without fear or intimidation *is* possible within a positive hierarchy, with horses and with children.**

clinic together, Big Mamma slowed at the trailer door then stepped right up and in. The two *partners* were on the road.

Should Big Mamma test Katie's resolve and leadership (and she will) by again refusing to get in the trailer, Katie won't get upset or angry because she's learned that horses naturally and regularly test for leadership and emotion has no place in discipline. Nor will she use force; she will consistently repeat the pattern of work, rest and reward until Mamma remembers that cooperation is where she'll find comfort.

This is how Katie used the Five Mighty C's to address her horse's problem behavior:

♡ She **considered** her own expectations and patterns of interaction with Big Mamma and what it was she wanted her to learn. She thought about Mamma's temperament and what motivated her. She used the challenge of the trailer as an *opportunity* to teach.

♡ She **connected** with Mamma's thinking brain using work and rest.

♡ Katie **communicated** her expectations consistently, clearly and fairly, so Big Mamma could *choose* to **co-operate.**

♡ She was **consistent** in her expectations and methods, helping Mamma to trust that she is a worthy leader.

Now, with Katie established as a fair and consistent leader, if they need to cross a bridge, go past a spooky object, or a horse-eating bunny hops by, Mamma will be more likely to trust that Katie has the matter confidently in hand and go forward per her request.

It's not hard to guess how Big Mamma would react should she again encounter that wrangler who forced her into the trailer. I'm sure we could see the whites of her eyes from the next county! He *could* get her in a trailer again and it might even be faster than the first time because she is fearful, but what of Mamma's confidence, her ability to connect to and trust humans? What would happen if *he* asked her to cross a bridge or they came across something spooky on a trail?

The goal for horses and for humans is self-control, not "I control you." Connection and cooperation without fear or intimidation, self-control, is nurtured within a positive hierarchy. A strong connection is what makes children and horses *want* to choose to do the right thing. This is where they find safety and comfort.

True discipline is teaching children to think and to learn. It's not force or punishment. Discipline is fair, thoughtful and respectful. The root of the word itself means, "to teach." Though a significant paradigm shift may be necessary in order to approach each expression of undesirable behavior as normal, expected and a valuable *opportunity* to teach, it will be one of the most important mental shifts you will make.

Those unpredictable and underappreciated "teachable moments" are rich opportunities to develop those elusive high level brain functions that we want our children to utilize when we are not around to guide them. We want positive integrated patterns firmly established in their brains when they're making decisions on their own in difficult and even dangerous, real world situations. The Five Mighty C's will help you recognize and use those teachable moments to your and your child's benefit!

"With discipline, punishment is unnecessary. Discipline is not a dirty word; it's the one thing that separates us from chaos and anarchy. It's not about making things happen. It's about supporting the horse's effort to get better. Discipline implies timing; it's the precursor to good behavior."

The intent of discipline is not to control the child, but to support a child's growth toward self-directed independence.

When you begin to view obnoxious behaviors as gifts of opportunity; when you *Take the Reins!* and embrace the Five Mighty C's, you can prevent your child's normal testing behaviors from becoming problem behaviors and raise respectful, resourceful and loving humans.

OK, Yeah... Children are Not Horses

To be clear, I am *not* saying that a child is the same as a horse and I am not promoting treating a child in exactly the same way you would a horse. This is as obvious to me as the warning on my new iron that states "Do not iron clothing while wearing." No, children are not 1000 pound beasts of burden, and we don't have identical ultimate goals for interacting.

Blind obedience is not what we want in our strong, responsible, independent, creatively thinking and problem solving children. When working with a horse, obedience without question or rarely a second thought on the part of the horse is a requirement – your life and/or intact body parts may depend on it. With a twenty-five pound iron-willed toddler, it may not be life or death, but more of a walk on the tightrope of sanity!

We *do,* however, want a positive, trusting relationship and willing cooperation with both horses and children. Obvious differences aside, because horses, unlike dogs or cats, are herd (not pack) and prey (not predator) animals, they are similar to our developing little humans in some critical and very relative ways.

They both:

- 🤍 Crave, test for, are inherently attuned to, relax, learn and develop their best potential within the comfort and safety of confident leadership.
- 🤍 Are brilliantly sensitive to every nuance of intent, emotion, attitude and body language.
- 🤍 Are not easily controlled. They require connection and clear, consistent communication in order to willingly cooperate.
- 🤍 They are honest. They give pure, unadulterated responses with no hidden agenda.
- 🤍 Learn from *everything* we do or say.
- 🤍 Are intuitive, reactive and "in the moment," requiring mindful awareness.
- 🤍 Are mirrors to our own souls and emotions.

Because of these similarities, horses, like our children, thrive within some of the same doctrines of discipline. There are profound benefits to employing the principles of interacting with these exquisitely sensitive, noble creatures. However, since not many parents can, or would want to get into a round pen with 1000 pounds of hooves and attitude in order to brush up on their parenting skills, this book will summarize the most beneficial and applicable parallels between "natural" horse training and positive parenting. The

> *Horses are amazing because they are sentient animals that mirror our personalities as well as our fears.*
> **Danielle Herb**

more horsemanship I learn, the more I realize that it isn't just a fun and clever way to present good parenting techniques; it has surprisingly applicable principles and unique insights to offer.

As the **Five Mighty C's** are explained in the following chapters, you'll find quotes from the horse whisperers in text boxes with this cowboy in them. The quotes are not credited to a specific person, because today's horsemen and women have drawn wisdom from a variety of related sources. One of my favorite horsemen, Richard Winters, simply says, "A wise old horseman once said _____." That about covers it.

My hope is that you will be pleasantly surprised how well the wisdom of the horse-whisperers applies to positive parenting and that this book will help you utilize their philosophies to improve your relationships with your children.

> If you *would* like to experience the amazing learning that can take place when working with horses, we provide experiential parenting workshops with horses – no riding involved – that are guaranteed to jump-start long term change. Send me an email!
> parentinghorsesense@gmail.com
>
> CONNECTED PARENTING

CHAPTER 2

REINS &
BRAINS

SOFT HANDS, STRONG REINS

As stated in the previous chapter, the underlying premise of *Take the Reins!* is strong leadership, with the parent-child relationship experienced as a **hierarchy** - parent at the top. Reins are my metaphor for the actions and interactions required to maintain a *loving* hierarchical relationship. The one who holds the reins takes responsibility for choosing direction and speed. You, the parent, are the one with the life experience to provide expectations and guidance. You are responsible for everything! Ground yourself in the strength of knowing that you, or the two of you, are meant to be the leader(s) in your herd. "Soft hands" on the reins means that you guide with wisdom, compassion, and balance.

"You should dispel the myth that you and your horse can be equal partners. One of you has to be dominant; it is either you or him. Your horse needs and wants you to be the benevolent leader of the herd. Horses are comfortable and happy when there is a true leader in the herd to keep order, offer guidance and keep them safe."

It is animal nature to function within a hierarchy. Remove competent leadership from any group, herd, pack or flock and a new hierarchy will form, even under bad leadership, as the human world has unfortunately experienced many times throughout history. Most animals willingly follow, feel safe and experience positive growth within good leadership.

Strong leadership does not equal being aggressive, mean or a tyrant. There is no need to jump from wimp to bully. You cannot force good behavior and have a positive relationship. Domineering insistence on obedience only breeds fear and resentment and slams closed the doors to communication.

Take the Reins! is an approach to disciplinary situations that expresses to your child with every fiber of your being, your voice, body language and expression that, **"I love you *and* I am in charge. There are no hard feelings; it's just the way it is."** The message should not be, "I love you, but *please* _____." The message should be a firm and matter-of-fact, "I love you, **and** you may not _____" or, "You must _____" or, "These are your choices _____."

Kids, like horses, are experts in detecting and exploiting weakness, *not* because they are evil power hungry monsters, but because they deeply crave the safety and comfort of strong leadership to the degree that if they detect a void in leadership, they will try to fill it. They *will* become power hungry monsters if forced to fill a void left by weak or inconsistent parenting!

Being a responsible and strong leader is hard work, especially when one is determined to keep connection, creativity and self-expression flourishing. Some parents fear that being the authority means they must use punishment in order to establish and enforce expectations, or that they could damage the delicate emerging psyche of their little darlin' by setting limits and enforcing rules. On the contrary, when expectations are developmentally appropriate and consistently enforced, children bloom with confidence! The Five Mighty C's will help you find and stay planted in the rich and rewarding middle ground.

> *Take the Reins!* **is a parental approach to disciplinary situations that expresses to your child with every fiber of your being, your voice, body language and expression that "I love you AND I am in charge."**

For many of you the idea that the parent-child relationship should be viewed as a hierarchy is a given, and you already see yourself as large and in charge. Yay for you - excellent first step! And there is so much more. I also ask you to define your strong leadership. How is it expressed in your relationship with your children? Is your leadership grounded in connection? I challenge you to openly and honestly consider, as you read on, if your approach strikes the *balance* between strength and gentle, loving support.

When expectations are developmentally appropriate and consistently enforced, children bloom with confidence!

A fear creeping around the recesses of any of any caring parent's mind are the more prevalent diagnoses of disorders such as ADD and ADHD and others. Parents must first be certain that their expectations, especially of little boys, are realistic. Typical children *need* to be active, play and run in order to develop normally, some more than others. But, if your gut is telling you something is just not right, then pursue an accurate diagnosis like a momma/papa bear.

I believe the principles of interaction presented here are effective and flexible enough to benefit most children regardless of a diagnosis. Set and work toward reasonable, individualized and attainable goals for your child. Specific techniques may have to be tweaked and your commitment and fortitude will be tested, but I have seen so many success stories, I'm convinced that these strategies can support positive outcomes for everyone.

The Different Brains

Before you pick up the reins, a little insight into the workings of the brain of that adorable beast of yours will help to clarify how and why the Five Mighty C's work. Current develop-mental brain research offers extraordinary new knowledge that should be

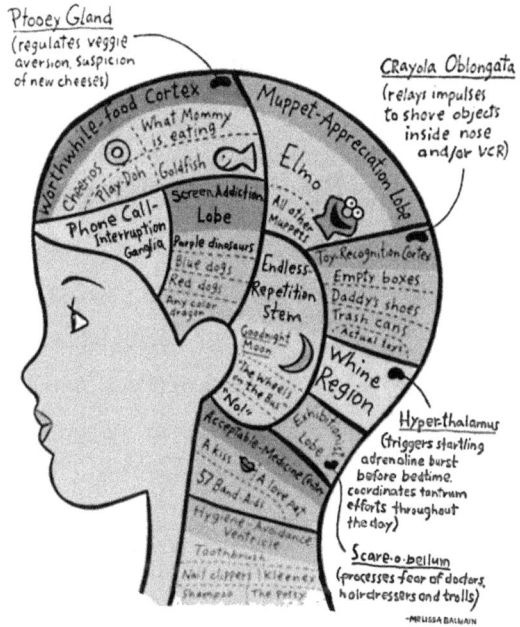

Ptooey Gland (regulates veggie aversion, suspicion of new cheeses)

CRayola Oblongata (relays impulses to shove objects inside nose and/or VCR)

Worthwhile-food Cortex · What Mommy is eating · Cheerios · Play-Doh · Goldfish

Muppet-Appreciation Lobe · Elmo · All other Muppets

Phone Call-Interruption Ganglia · Screen Addiction Lobe · Purple dinosaurs · Blue dogs · Red dogs · Any color dragon

Endless Repetition Stem

Toy-Recognition Cortex · Empty boxes · Daddy's shoes · Trash cans · "Actual toys"

Goodnight Moon · "The wheels on the bus" · "No!s"

Whine Region

Hyperthalamus (triggers startling adrenaline burst before bedtime. coordinates tantrum efforts throughout the day)

Acceptable-Medicine Center · A kiss · A love Pat · Exhibition Lobe · $7 Band-Aid

Hygiene-Avoidance Ventricle · Toothbrush · Nail clippers · Kleenex · Shampoo · The Potty

Scare-o-bellum (processes fear of doctors, hairdressers and trolls)

—MELISSA BALMAIN

helpful for parents, but can be a bit daunting when attempting to apply it to everyday adult-child interactions. The principles and strategies in *Take the Reins!* are informed by this research and are designed to help with its practical application.

Science now confirms what parents and teachers have long recognized; everything that happens to us, all our experiences from in utero on, such as how the people in our circle of care respond to us, how we are disciplined, the music we hear, what we read, what we spend time doing, not only profoundly affect character, but the actual organic development of the brain. This development is the result of normal brain growth and the process of creating and strengthening the connections or synapses between the cells of the brain, wiring and re-wiring according to experience. Frequently used pathways become stronger and denser while synapses that are not used become weakened, inactive and are eventually "pruned" away. This process goes on constantly throughout life. The younger the brain, the more elastic it is, with the majority of the pruning taking place *before age three.*

Here are a few examples of how research says real parents with real kids can facilitate this process in positive ways:

- ♡ Talking and responding to a baby a lot *significantly* speeds up the process of learning language. The number of words a child has in his vocabulary when entering kindergarten has been shown to be a reliable predictor of success in school.

- ♡ Screen time – baby videos, watching TV, playing video games, etc., will wire the brain in certain ways, many of them negative. The more screen time a child experiences, the less he is able to engage in self-directed play and the more screen time he needs to keep himself entertained. A finding of particular concern showed evidence of too much screen time damaging an area of the brain known as the *insula,* which is involved in our capacity to develop empathy and compassion for others and the ability to integrate physical signals with emotion. These skills dictate the depth and quality of personal relationships and a lack of them has been linked to violent behavior (Zhou 2011, Yuan 2011, Weng 2013, and Weng 2012). Physical activity, music, creative endeavors and face to face interactions help to wire the brain in ways that promote positive intellectual and emotional growth.

- ♡ Emotions develop and build in layers, each more complex than the last. Children whose parents talk with them about their feelings in everyday conversations can understand their own and other's emotions more fully and tend to develop higher levels of emotional intelligence and empathy. Seeing adults positively resolve conflict is more beneficial to emotional development than not seeing conflict at all.

♡ Given the opportunity to practice age appropriate decision making, children learn to make good decisions.

♡ Given the opportunity to be bored, children learn to entertain themselves, build creativity and the ability to mentally dive deeply into social and independent play which translates into the ability to mentally dive deeply into relationships, projects and work in later life.

As you work to improve your parent-child interactions and ultimately your child's mind, here is a generalized, but useful description of some portions of this spongy new brain relevant to using the strategies that will be presented in *Take the Reins!*:

1. There is the primitive lower brain, the "reptilian" brain whose purpose is survival, food, escape, attack.

2. The upper cortex houses the frontal lobes that are involved in higher level thinking - executive functions such as the formation of decisions, planning, learning, controlling impulses, and perspective taking. These frontal lobes are divided into left and right hemispheres.

    a. The right hemisphere is holistic, non-verbal, emotional, and intuitive. It is experiential and more influenced by the body and lower brain.

    b. The left brain is logical, linear, linguistic, and literal.

Ideally, survival instincts, emotions and logical thought work together, with the evolved upper cortex in charge most of the time. The younger the child, the more he or she functions within the lower and right brain and the less they are able to reason. The goal for parents is to build an integrated brain that can flexibly rebalance when one portion dominates and where the different areas of the brain communicate with each other faster than teenagers can text. We want to *intentionally* build the developing cortex in ways that promote those high level executive functions. Domineering or lazy parenting can create lasting patterns of rigidity and dependence on portions of the brain that negatively influence a child's future ability to engage in positive relationships, learn, and make good decisions. Connection and integration is the goal.

For more in-depth knowledge about developing your child's integrated brain, I highly recommend the excellent book, *The Whole Brain Child* by Daniel Seigel and Tina Bryson. They offer more specific techniques to develop the logical, reasoning, empathetic, and joyful brain of your child. They emphasize that, "The brain is significantly shaped by the experiences we offer as parents!"

The Five Mighty C's are designed to guide you in facilitating integration, connection and optimal brain develop-ment through positive discipline. As you begin to put these principles to work in your everyday life, they will create frequently used synapses in your own brain that will keep you dancing in the authori*tative* middle ground of parenting. Not too tough and not too wimpy!

What's Your Reining Style?

How do you know if you are balanced – a strong *and* loving leader? In the horse world we call this skill having "great hands" on the reins. We strive for effective reining with steady connection and a gentle, light touch. To know if you have great hands, let's start with a brief overview of the long established differences between authori*tarian*, permissive, and authori*tative* parenting styles and the effects of each.

The Tyrant - Authoritarian parents can be overly critical and rejecting. To exert their constant need to control they yell, command, criticize, and threaten; "Do it because I said so" is the prevailing attitude. They make decisions *for* their child and expect him or her to accept their dictates without question; they force and punish the child when she or he resists. (Hands too heavy on the reins.)

The Flower Child - Permissive parents coddle, overindulge, are indecisive, don't pay attention to, or are manipulated by their

child, showing little or no control. Instead of gradually granting autonomy and independence as the child gains competence, they let their child make decisions before he or she is capable; i.e., children of permissive parents may eat meals, go to bed and watch TV whenever they want. ("What are reins?")

The Dancer - Authoritative parents balance insisting on mature behavior and offering reasons for their expectations, with using disciplinary encounters as teachable moments to promote their child's self-regulation. They engage in gradual, appropriate granting of autonomy, supporting their child in learning to make decisions when she or he is developmentally ready. They are warm, attentive, and sensitive to their child's temperament and establish an emotionally fulfilling parent-child relationship that draws the child into a close connection. At the same time, they exercise firm, reasonable control. (A responsive and soft touch on the reins.)

The Dr. Jekyll/Mr. Hyde - Combination parent is inconsistent. This is my own addition to the traditionally accepted three categories above. It is born from observing real parents interact with real children over the years and, ugh yes, from some of my own parenting experiences. Here, there is lack of consistency in responses to behavior. One time a child misbehaves, he is ignored, another time he is soundly punished – usually with an explosion of emotion. The reins are either way too short or way too long with no discernable logic as to when either is to be expected. Consider the unfortunate child who has Dr. Jekyll and Mrs. Hyde as parents! What skill sets might he develop in order to survive in his unpredictable world?

There is clear and sobering research about the long term effects of the different child-rearing styles. That said, it is important to acknowledge that there are vast differences in the temperaments of children and that the mismatch of temperament between parent and child can create communication challenges for both parties. There are an infinite number of reasons relationships go awry. The principles and strategies presented in this book are meant to be a framework for interacting that brings out the best in parents and children, they are not meant to inspire guilt. The following are research-based generalities, not indictments. Here's how it shakes out:

Children raised by **authoritarian** parents tend to be anxious, unhappy, have low self-esteem and lack self-reliance; they often react with defiance, anger and force when frustrated. They tend to either be bullies or followers. The child whose coping strategies emulate a model of handling conflict with punishment or force becomes the bully. Children who are denied the chance to make appropriate decisions on their own and who live a pattern of listening to others to tell them what to do may become perpetual victims. Both tend to be quick to blame others, unforgiving and bitter.

"If you allow a horse to make mistakes, the horse will learn from his mistakes no different than the human. But you can't get him to where he dreads making mistakes for fear of what's going to happen after he does."

> **Children raised with permissiveness or lack of appropriate parental involvement and connection, regardless of the reason behind it, are more likely to use addictive behaviors to bail themselves out of bad moods or situations.**

The children of **permissive** parents are prone to being impulsive, rebellious, manipulative and disobedient; they may also be overly demanding, whiny, dependent on adults, and less persistent with challenges, expecting applause every time they do the tiniest task. They can develop an entitled mindset with the learned thought pattern, "It's all about me." "Someone will/should do things for me." Children raised with permissiveness or lack of appropriate parental involvement and connection, regardless of the reason behind it, are more likely to use addictive behaviors to bail themselves out of bad moods or situations.

Children raised in an **authoritative** household tend towards an upbeat mood, self-control, task persistence, cooperativeness, high self-esteem, confidence and take responsibility for their own behavior.

For the **Combination style**, it depends on a child's temperament. He or she may internalize the inconsistency by becoming withdrawn, anxious, fearful or angry, or take the aggressive, defiant or manipulative route for coping. None of the results are good.

When more than one person is responsible for childrearing decisions, whether they reside in the same household or not, all parties must be in relative agreement on their approaches to discipline. The proven negative results of inconsistency are why it is so important for divorced parents to put the child's psychological needs ahead of their own need to be right, for revenge, or to vie for the love and approval of the children. Co-parents must do some ground work together and find common ground in their expectations of the children and their goals for parenting if the children are to develop healthy behavior patterns and emotionally healthy lives.

Because parents as well as their children have real lives and a broad spectrum of temperaments, normal human differences in delivery of discipline are to be expected. In order to minimize children's confusion and/or ability to use manipulation as a control strategy, parents must work to find relative agreement on basic family rules and present a united front. One of the most important *and* most difficult principles of *Take the Reins!* is consistency.

It doesn't take a child psychologist to figure out the most effective and recommended method of parenting. The Five Mighty C's will keep you dancing in the authorit*ative* middle ground, neither too rigid, limiting expression, creativity and problem solving, nor too permissive, allowing chaos to thrive.

When you tackle the important work of grounding yourself in familiar, workable principles, you become mentally and emotionally fit, less reactive, worried or guilty, so that you can say and do the right thing at the right time for the right results. Authoritative parenting *is* within every parent's grasp.

Practice Makes Perfect – ish

In order to effectively put new principles and strategies to practical use and create positive lasting change, one must practice. Current brain research shows that even in the adult brain, practice, whether mentally rehearsing scenarios or practicing aloud with others, creates actual physical connections, synapses, and patterns in the brain that make it easier to use those patterns when you really need them. We now have proof that visualization practice does make, if not perfect, a whole lot better each time.

> *"Not surprisingly, I'm all for the authoritative approach when it comes to horses and children. I can say from personal experience that permissive parenting has major drawbacks. I don't think my son, now 21, would take kindly to a round pen and a lunge line, but I wish I'd understood the child-rearing equivalent of natural horsemanship when he was young. We both would have learned important lessons in boundary-setting, attentiveness, responsibility, and cooperation—and we might even have avoided a certain unpleasant visit to juvenile court."*
> **Parenting Workshop Attendee**

Practicing on your live children is a bit like practicing catching a bullet in your teeth; you want to get it right the first time. When those teachable moments arise, you will be grateful that you rehearsed appropriate responses so they are at the tip of your tongue (or your cortex) instead of acting on the first reaction that slides from your reptile brain. A practiced response can derail an impending war while teaching skillful communication.

In this book practice activities are called **"Ground Work."** This term comes from the essential prep work good horse trainers do with their horses, usually in an approximately sixty foot round arena, before ever stepping into the saddle. This work gets horse and rider connected and focused on each other's cues and expectations for the ride to come. The Ground Work activities offered here are meant to increase your understanding of the principle or strategy being presented, give you meaningful skills and tools (no whips or spurs) and enlightening, sometimes even fun, ways to practice those skills.

Most Ground Work activities can be completed in less than a half hour, however, to get the maximum benefit from each exercise, take your time. Reflect and write down your answers to questions. The Five Mighty C's are not meant to be a quick fix, but a change in thinking and approach to childrearing. It can take months, even years to shift family dynamics for the long haul. Know that he time you choose to spend doing the ground work is a true gift to yourself and to your family.

Create lasting change by making small changes, gradually merging them into your everyday interactions with your children. For the most consistent results, if you are part of a caregiving partnership, do the work as a team, save your answers and refer back to them. If that isn't an option, share your discoveries and intended changes with a friend or family member.

This process is not meant to add to your parenting stress level, it is meant to help you feel confident and self-assured in your interactions. Recognize and appreciate every small success and when you're ready, move on to another ground work session at a pace that suits your family. Change shakes your foundation, showering the previously comfortable pieces of your psyche down in sometimes uncomfortable new places and patterns. It's more likely to stick if you take it slow and make it enjoyable by taking the time to acknowledge your own, each other's and your children's efforts and accomplishments.

> **You are not only making your life easier and your children's lives richer and more successful; you are influencing how future generations of your family will parent *their* children.**

You can count on the unfortunate wisdom of that old saying, "It'll get worse before it gets better" as you become a stronger leader and are more consistent in your enforcement of rules and expectations. Don't give up! When you meet resistance, you'll know you're on the right track. Keep at it! The long term results will be worth your persistence. You are not only making your life easier and your children's lives richer and more successful; you are influencing how future generations of your family will parent *their* children. *Take the Reins* and let's start down that trail!

Here are the top 10 parenting lessons horses have taught me:

1. *Sleep is a luxury, not a necessity.*
2. *I'll be the one cleaning up the manure in this relationship.*
3. *Come rain, sleet, sickness or snow, there are no days off from this job.*
4. *There is no room for emotions in discipline.*
5. *Success is fleeting; it's the ride that counts.*
6. *A little dirt never killed anyone.*
7. *Every day is a new opportunity to screw them up.*
8. *They will surprise and delight and terrify you on daily basis.*
9. *A sense of humor is a job requirement.*
10. *I'll probably never quite figure out this job.*

Horsewoman & Mother of Two

"*Analytical thought and the power of observation are the greatest tools in the realm of horse training. You must think and observe. If you think like a horse, it will be easier to form a relationship. You have to be the one to make the effort to learn to think empathetically, it is impossible for a horse.*"

CHAPTER 3

PRINCIPLE 1, CONSIDER

"You have to get discipline within yourself so that you can have it with your horse. To be effective, teaching must be intentional."

BEFORE YOU PICK UP THE REINS, HERE ARE THREE THINGS TO CONSIDER:

1. Your Goals

When you pick up the reins, it helps to know where you're headed. Yogi Berra said, "If you don't know where you're going, you'll end up some place else." Not a good plan for raising kids! The first step in moving toward a loving, hierarchal parent/child relationship is defining what your goals are for your child.

In the life changing and insightful book *Crucial Conversations, Tools for Talking When the Stakes are High*, the authors, Patterson, Grenny, McMillan, and Switzler, provide strategies to improve one's dialogue skills when conversations turn crucial. Their criteria for defining a crucial conversation are:

- ♡ Opinions vary
- ♡ The stakes are high
- ♡ Emotions run strong

Sounds to me like most family conversations! The format and results of these types of conversations have a huge impact on your family's quality of life. However, we often either avoid them out of aversion to confrontation or fear of making the situation worse, or we simply handle them badly. We yell, demand, withdraw, resort to sarcasm or silence and say or do things we regret, or should regret.

Even if we are determined to handle a conversation or confrontation productively, we may not have experienced the best examples of how to communicate in a way that promotes a win-win result. When the going gets tough, we fall back on learned patterns that may or may not serve our long-term goals for our children. Most of us have learned, "Win at all cost," or my personal go-to favorite, "Avoid at all cost." We are often our own worst enemy, creating and then repeating an unhealthy, self-defeating loop while unintentionally teaching our children to interact in exactly the same way.

> **We are often our own worst enemy, creating and then repeating an unhealthy, self-defeating loop while teaching our children to interact in exactly the same way.**

The authors of *Crucial Conversations* cite twenty years of research involving more than 100,000 people, showing that the key skill of the most effective leaders, teammates, parents and loved ones is the capacity to skillfully address emotionally and politically risky issues. Their research shows that people who can skillfully master crucial conversations:

♡ Have more successful careers, are more influential, can get things done and build lasting relationships.

♡ Are healthier, with stronger immune systems and a longer life.

♡ Are happier with more satisfying, close relationships that are maintained over time.

As you work through Ground Work 1, defining goals for your children, consider some of the words used in these three bullets as a starting point; successful, healthy, happy, close relationships. You have ahead of you an opportunity to build into your children the foundation of character and life skills necessary to thrive in a complex, fast moving, changing and uncertain world. By interacting in ways that build children's executive functions such as self-awareness (including a willingness to acknowledge one's own mistakes and grow from them), mindfulness, understanding another's perspective, connectedness, and an ability to focus on problem solving as opposed to blaming others, you can grow their brains in a way that minimizes their need to *learn* to communicate positively as adults. What a gift you can give! And it's not just a gift to your child; think how grateful a future spouse, children, friends and co-workers will be!

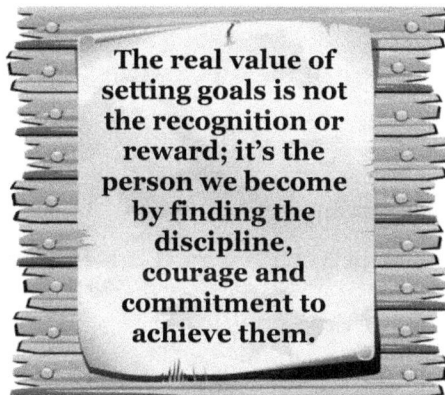

> **The real value of setting goals is not the recognition or reward; it's the person we become by finding the discipline, courage and commitment to achieve them.**

Ground Work 1 – Who Will I Be?

On one piece of paper write the first six words that come to your mind to describe yourself and set them aside. Be honest!

- Now, close your eyes and imagine your child as an adult. On a separate paper write *at least fifteen* characteristics that you would use to describe that person you see and goals for his/her life.

- Next, shorten the list to the six most important characteristics or goals. There are two purposes to this part of the exercise. One is to identify and clarify your own values and expectations. The other is to remind you to ask yourself, any time you are intentionally teaching or disciplining your child, whether you are helping him to become more _____. (Fill in the blank with one of your final six characteristics.) **This will tell you whether you are doing what you are doing *for* him or *to* him, and whether you are responding or reacting to his behavior**. Consider how much time you spend intentionally thinking about and acting toward developing these qualities in your children.

- Finally, look back at the list of words you used to describe yourself. If they are the same words you used to describe your child/future adult - fantastic! If not, remember you are always teaching your child to become who you are.

2. Your Child

Of course, I realize that you know your own child or children better than you know every bump, lump and bit of beauty on your own body. *And,* I'm going to ask you to channel your inner scientist and dig even deeper in order to *objectively* observe them in different circumstances and without emotion. It's helpful if you can also have a trusted friend, relative or teacher observe and report back to you.

Dedicate some uninterrupted, focused time toward analyzing your child's interactions with different people in different environments and situations. Remove yourself from the interaction equation so you can really see, hear and sense life from your child's point of view. Answer questions such as:

- ♡ In new situations, is he anxious, hesitant, calm, or fearless?
- ♡ Faced with a difficult task, does she persist in finding solutions before asking for help?
- ♡ Is he easily frustrated, if so, what specifically triggers that frustration?
- ♡ How is she comforted when upset, sad or disappointed?
- ♡ What are his favorite ways to test you?

For infants, study their cues – their cries, movements, head turns, kicks, bracing, and preferred touch. With young children, examine their fears, frustrations and likes. What will instantly get a, "No!" reaction? What stimulates and what over-stimulates them? What comforts and calms them? Do they learn best visually, auditorily, or by doing? (I always said my youngest had to pee on the electric fence; I couldn't tell him anything! Still can't.) And with older children, discover what makes them curious, what lights them up. How do they handle boredom? In what ways do your two temperaments complement each other and how do they aggravate each other? What rules are they most likely to ignore or defy?

Remove the filter of what you want for them. Quiet your own expectations and dreams to uncover what theirs are. Is it science, nature, technology, books, competition, dance, pretending, music, math, building, taking things apart, riding horses? What type of communication do they respond to positively/negatively? Can you identify a pattern in *their* re-actions to your reactions?

Objectively investigate why misbehavior occurs, without emotion or blame. Consider if a changing behavior is due to entering a new developmental stage. Be open to possibilities you haven't previously considered and don't assume *anything*. Might you be assigning your own feelings to your child? Is her schedule or routine not fitting her changing needs? Is a request developmentally in-appropriate? Is he confused, frustrated or does he lack the skills to cope or to do what is expected? Is he tired or coming down with a bug? Is she simply testing your limits and resolve?

> *"You must learn why he does what he does. Learn to predict- 'Figure out what happened before what happened happened.'"*

After any incident, take time to answer, "What happened before what happened, happened" (not a typo - old horseman's saying). Try to identify patterns. Your efforts will pay off in droves by helping you predict unwanted behavior so you can choose responses, words and consequences that teach positive lessons and prevent future misbehavior.

Discover what calms your child and what encourages him to connect to you at each age and stage of his development. This is not a one-time activity; your strategies must evolve as he matures. Even though basic temperament will not usually change wildly through the years, the specifics of what works will need to be re-examined. That hug that worked to get him connected to you at four will guarantee an eye roll and quick retreat at fourteen! You'll need to update this vital information through the years in order to make that essential connection to the thinking side of your child's brain.

Note that the intent of this investigation is not to figure out how to change your child's nature; you do it to understand his nature and to know how best to support his development. Getting to know the particulars of his individual temperament will also teach him that he is worth learning about.

Hooray for Testing!

Your child's testing behaviors are golden opportunities! Mark Rashid said, "There can't be comfort without a little discomfort, and there can't be balance unless things become a little

unbalanced." It is the *job* of horses *and* children to test their limits! Each age and stage of development has its own expression of testing behavior and every human being differs in amount, style and intensity, but recognize that **children do not initially misbehave out of malice.** It's the adults in the relationship that have the power to turn any situation into a W.W.F. match – or not.

Children come to us with a range of temperaments, innate abilities and potential, but they do *not* come to us magically knowing the rules and customs of the society and family they are born into. Nor are they inherently evil *or* angelic. There is no such thing as a bad baby. Typical kids are raw human nature, just exactly as it should be. They must test those in their circle of care to find out what the accepted rules and customs of this new life are. Your actions, words and attitude define for them who they are in their new world.

> **Your actions, words and attitude define for your children who they are in their new world.**

Embrace this fact and you will boost your ability to see your child as a perfect bundle of potential, and you'll set yourself up to respond unemotionally when confronted with his/her repertoire of testing behaviors. When you view misbehavior as healthy, natural attempts to explore the norms of this mysterious new environment, it's easier to stay calm and not react as if the behavior is meant as a personal challenge. Only then can you begin to perceive your child saying "No," ignoring you, whining and even defiance as an opportunity to cement your leadership and to teach.

> *"In difficulty there is oppor-tunity."*

Familiarize yourself with the typical physical and emotional milestones of your child's age and developmental level. Family values and rules must be fair and developmentally appropriate. As we explore allowing your child to make mistakes and learn from failures, it is important that those challenges are appropriate; you don't want to promote the message that he is a failure by setting him up for constant failure! He has to experience successes along the way in order to learn to succeed. Your goal is to be the sage, the wise one who provides coaching and supports the development of perseverance in the face of challenges!

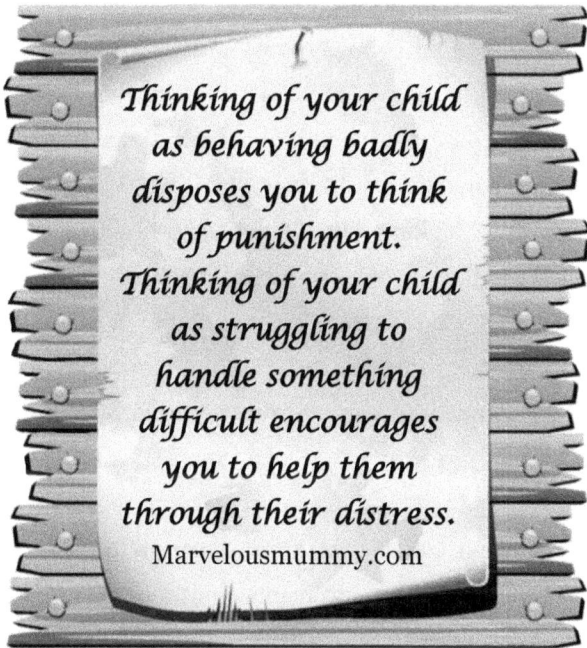

Thinking of your child as behaving badly disposes you to think of punishment. Thinking of your child as struggling to handle something difficult encourages you to help them through their distress.
Marvelousmummy.com

Ground Work 2 – Channel Your Inner Scientist

- Write down *exactly* what you see and/or hear as you observe your child three different times in one day for 10-15 minutes each. You should not be interacting, just observing.

- Try to view different situations; give your child a new toy and observe how he explores it alone. Have another person interact with him. Watch him interact with other children.

- Do not assume or use judgmental words, write only facts. If you are writing phrases like, "She was angry," ask yourself how you knew she was angry, and then write those words instead. This will help you to observe objectively.

For example, which observation would give you the most useful information about your child, #1 or #2?

1. When Ralph took Henry's truck, Henry yelled, "No! It's mine!" Then he slumped his shoulders and started to cry.
2. Henry got angry when Ralph took his truck away.

1. Becky stood looking down, quiet when Mom said, "Goodbye." When Mom was out the door, Becky turned, smiled and joined her friends in the play house.
2. Becky wasn't really sad when her mom left today.

You will be surprised how much you can learn by looking through an objective lens! With some practice, you will be able to think back on an incident – a tantrum, an argument, an outburst - and know **"what happened before what happened, happened."** Then you can use the information to plan ahead to prevent problems and respond with teaching in mind.

On Developmental Appropriateness

When planning to implement the Five Mighty C's, it is important to remember that the younger the child, the more he reacts emotionally to any fear or frustration and the harder it may be to calm or reason with him. Consider a stimulus; say a large dog barks loudly near a child of different ages:

♡ A young infant will startle, immediately cry and may be difficult to console. He is functioning entirely within the primitive, emotional portions of his brain.

♡ A toddler over a year of age may also cry, but will look to the people around her for cues as to how to react. The reasoning, social portions of her brain are developing and she can be comforted by her caregiver.

♡ A preschooler who has developed language and a base of experiences with dogs will evaluate the situation based on those experiences and may retreat behind mom, but can express his fear or curiosity and be reassured using words.

The refined, logical portions of the brain that allow a child to reason and problem solve, grow with maturity and our support. Parents know from experience though, that a child's behavior at any given moment can be an expression of the brain's primitive level responses and age does not always dictate reasonableness! As the caretakers of these immature brains, we must interact with knowledge and awareness of the child's developmental level, temperament and portion of their brain that is controlling their behavior at any given moment. We must constantly reassess the developmental appropriateness of expectations.

3. You

It's never the horse's fault and...it's never the child's fault. Do you feel a little gag reflex on that big 'ol pill? You're not alone. Looking objectively at yourself and your own expectations and patterns of interaction is admittedly amazingly hard to do with honesty. But, if your goal is to help your child develop and learn to maximize the use of *his* cortex, you have to do the same. Opening yourself up to objective self-examination *can* be an empowering experience if you put your open and objective heart into the job.

> *"Look first to your own behavior in working with a 'problem horse.' It's never the horse's fault!"*

First, consider if you truly embrace the concept that the fundamental relationship with your child should be a hierarchy. Is this idea a comfortable fit, or does it need some closer examination, some questions to be asked and answered? Is it balanced with love and connection? Does it hold up under the pressure of a two year old's tantrum, a four year old's whining fit or a nine year old's arguing? Perceived weakness, self-doubt or lack of consistency are a recipe for turning normal testing behaviors into any number of narcissistic, entitled or helpless victim types of personality disorders.

"For horses, a sense of safety comes from being in the presence of a truly alpha leader, an individual who is confident, aware of the environment, in charge and in control. An individual, who states and enforces rules, is fair and consistent, provides structure and meaning to an otherwise chaotic world."

Get objectively curious about *your* typical reactions to confrontation, defiance or crucial conversations.

- ♡ Is guilt covertly motivating any of your disciplinary decisions?
- ♡ Do you show anger first and ask questions after? Or do you not even ask questions?
- ♡ Do you take comments personally, use sarcasm or are silence and withdrawal your preferred M.O.?
- ♡ Do you actively listen and are you truly empathetic?

♡ Do you make assumptions about other's motivations based on your own experiences?

♡ Do you give attention to unwanted behaviors? Even negative attention counts as attention.

♡ Are you reacting in the same way your parents did? If so, close your eyes and take a mental voyage back in time and remember how the way you were disciplined made you feel when you were a child. Give the emotions names and consider what you *really* learned from how you were parented. Examine and appreciate everything that brought you to where you are now.

Think of a recent conflict where you felt you achieved your desired outcome, then take your reflection a step further and ask yourself:

♡ What did my child learn from me during that incident about how relationships should work?

♡ Did I listen and understand my child's point of view?

♡ Did I help identify feelings?

♡ Did I try for and achieve a "win"?

♡ Did I keep a goal for teaching in mind?

♡ What unintentional lessons may have been learned?

♡ Was there unresolved resentment and anger?

♡ Did I react or respond?

If you felt you responded appropriately, reflect on why you chose the action you did. What was your decision based on? Could you have done anything differently so the event ended in additional positive learning experiences? You're not asking these questions to weaken or undermine your confidence as a parent, but to build and maintain momentum toward improvement.

Identify your negative behavior triggers. Does whining send razor blades up your spine? It sure did mine! Does your child's "No!" turn you into a charging bear? Does being ignored make you want to get their attention with a two by four? Again, investigate "what happened before what happened, happened," only this time with a mirror. Examine your reactions with inquisitiveness. Give yourself the emotional space to really feel the emotions without criticism. When you identify patterns of interaction that show room for improvement, become a compassionate and objective scientist and say to yourself, "Isn't that interesting!" not, "I'm a bad parent."

This self-knowledge is the first step toward building your ability to routinely experience mindful awareness of your own reactions. Emotional awareness can help you slow down and buy the time you may need to recognize a behavior as an opportunity to teach something positive instead of an unintentional, possibly destructive lesson.

After you acknowledge the presence of your reactive emotions and have narrowed down what triggers them, experiment with what it takes to control your response to them. Visualize and rehearse those same emotions followed by an intentional response of your *choice*. When you feel that rising anger...take a deep breath. About to retreat into silence...ask a question. See yourself making a response not a reaction. Mentally rehearse your new responses often to strengthen those synapses. Be kind to yourself. You've taken a courageous look down a trail where many parents won't even take a peek. *Never stop reflecting and evolving.*

What are your boundaries? *Take the Reins!* offers a set of principles to serve as a framework for your adult-child interactions, but the specifics of acceptable and unacceptable behaviors, *your* boundaries, are up to you. Make reasonable, developmentally appropriate, fair and thoughtful choices. Consider your expectations of yourself and of your children with as much kindness and specificity as possible. Carefully consider family culture, interactions, routines, chores, mealtimes, bedtimes, screen time, etc. Defining these rules of engagement should be a lifelong, ongoing process as your family matures and evolves (Chapter 6).

This step is even more important today because of the unprecedented amount of choice available in modern society. In the past, expectations were at least partially dictated by family, the church, and the community. Families are exposed to so much more diversity in behavior in this growing media enhanced global community, that parents must consider a much wider variety of decisions regarding their children's behavior. As you become familiar with the Five Mighty C's, visualize how they will typically look in action with you and your family. Rehearse them in your mind. Make them yours; they should reflect your family's values, culture and unique personalities.

> **In order to mature with true self-esteem, children need a parent who is secure and confident in their personhood and parenthood.**

Whether you want to make major changes or just tweak a few existing strategies, don't expect instant and perfect transformation! You may want to start out by *"Acting as if."* Play the part. Act as if your children were being parented by Gandhi, Dr. Phil, or your grandmother! Know that you will make mistakes; congratulate yourself for recognizing them and move on. Change is a difficult and lifelong process. Pat yourself on the back when you've handled an event or any portion of an event particularly well. If you have a parenting partner, notice and mention their positive interactions as well.

When you've done your self-reflection, clarified your family values, goals and expectations and embraced a set of principles that fit comfortably in your psyche, you will be equipped to perform that incredible balancing act, being a strong *and* loving parent.

Ground Work 3 – Feel Your History (Small box – huge importance!)

Take plenty of time to think about and write down each answer. This is a must-do activity for two-parent families. Discuss with a friend or partner.

- Write down 5-10 bullet points that describe how you were parented, the great and the not so great. Include discipline, communication, routines, chores, displays of affection.
- In as much detail and clarity as you can, describe how each point made you feel. Putting time and thought into this part will help you understand your own behavior triggers.
- Consider how it affects your parenting today. What do you do that is the same? Which patterns are serving to promote positive behavior and learning in your children? Which are not?
- If you did not experience all positive examples of how to create conversations that are connected and end in a win-win, or to handle discipline positively, consider and create a list of specific steps you will commit to practicing in order to make that happen as you read though the rest of this book.

On Guilt

Undesirable behaviors are expressed by children with differing abilities and temperaments and from all walks of life, from poor families, rich families and everything in-between, in children raised by single parents, two parents, co-parents, grandparents, at home and working parents and from every orientation, culture and ethnicity. The one consistent factor I've observed as a culprit in escalating unwanted behavior in children is when their parent has slipped into the mucky, complicated quagmire of guilt.

Guilt can cause parents to doubt their disciplinary decisions creating inconsistency, lack of clear boundaries, and a parent who is all too often being manipulated. Regardless of the origin, a child or parent's illness or special needs, addiction, poverty, divorce, lack of time spent with the children, an absence, or any other cause, guilt can undermine confidence.

The sad irony is, it's even more critical that parents in challenging circumstances be grounded in strong, positive parenting principles that are consistently implemented in order to provide the safety and security children in vulnerable situations desperately need. It's important to openly and honestly examine your own emotions and motivations in order to respond in a way that will teach positive lessons.

"I believe that the best way to inspire a quality, or even a habit, in our kids is to cultivate it in ourselves. This means that parenting is a constant journey of learning and growth, or looking outward, toward my children, to see the areas in which I need to work at improving myself."

Hannah Guari Ma

"Rules without relationship = rebellion.
It takes time and effort to establish and build a relationship. If you try to lead them without loving them, you'll fail them."

CHAPTER 4

PRINCIPLE 2, CONNECT

"A horse doesn't care how much you know, until he knows how much you care."

PICK UP THE REINS

Connect to Build the Relationship

The profound wisdom of the famous horseman, Buck Brannaman's phrase "Rules without relationship equals rebellion" cannot be stressed enough. He continues, "If you skip the relationship building part or minimize it, or marginalize it, the idea, the very purpose of discipline is only half-baked and will not work."

Building and maintaining a connected, hierarchal relationship doesn't automatically happen because you exist in the same environment, provide life's necessities, and direct your children in doing the right thing. "Quality Time" is not just a catch phrase. Well, it is, but, the time you spend engaged *with* and not directing or correcting your child is what builds your relationship.

Picture your message of strength delivered in an envelope of love. There must be a loving foundational relationship in place

> **Picture your message of strength delivered in an envelope of love.**

in order for your child to hear you, respect you, and accept your leadership. Maintaining the balance between being a strong, consistent leader and being fair, loving and connected is not an endeavor for the lazy, distracted or guilty. It is not for those looking for easy answers or quick fixes. It takes constant nurturing, self-reflection and willingness to grow. The balancing act required for truly responsible parenting is the hardest, most painful, infuriating, joyous, amazing, rewarding job you will ever love! And it's 24/7 for the rest of your life. Know that when you work the balance of love and strength, you build a lifetime of connection.

One way to assure that uninterrupted, relationship building, quality time happens is to plan for it, calendar it and make it a sacred priority, not an "if I have time" item. Use your objective observations to learn about your children's favorite activities (not what *you* would like for those activities to be), then participate in them by *following their lead*. Give them a choice in what you do together and let them set the pace and direction of the activity or play. Get on the floor, in the sandbox or in the blanket fort and

pretend, be silly, get dirty, dress up, *whatever it takes!* Ask questions and listen. They need you to turn off the phone and the TV, unplug, shut off the to-do recording in your brain and *engage!* You love your kids...let them experience it.

Taking your kids to practice, helping with homework, sharing a meal are all good opportunities to converse and to build your relationship, but I'm referring here to carving out some child-directed time where you are totally present and focused.

When you nurture a connected relationship, you *should* expect your child to comply with your well-considered expectations. You are not being a Tyrant. The techniques discussed in this and the next three chapters are designed specifically to strengthen your parent-child connection.

> *"To get the horse in a more compliant frame of mind, get him connected to you (sometimes referred to as "Join-up"). He has to trust you and accept your leadership. Only then can you ask for more obedient behavior."*

> **Your kids need you to turn off the phone and the TV, unplug, shut off the to-do recording in your brain and engage! You love your kids...let them experience it.**

Ground Work 4 – Create "We"

- *With* your child or children, make a list of all their favorite activities, people and places. In one article I read, the family did this at the beginning of each summer and called it a "Summer Bucket List." It eliminated a lot of guilt for the mom because she found the activities her children came up with were not extravagant things like going to Disneyland, but simple, fun and accessible things like having a water-balloon fight!

- From the list, choose five activities that you feel like you will enjoy doing with your child(ren). In order to reduce stress and keep it simple, try to select common, preferably free activities, for example: go to the park, read, walk, talk, garden, play in the dirt, play in the water, build forts, play dress up, draw, cook, blow bubbles, color, sing, do puzzles, ride bikes, roller skate, play hide 'n seek, whatever "gets" *your* kid. Update the list as your child ages.

- Calendar these activities, make them a priority, and do them! Start with two items from your list per week, then build up to at least one per day. With multiple kids, try to fit in unique one-on-one sessions as often as possible.

- If you already do this, good for you! Make it even richer by reflecting on which activities your child most enjoyed, what got him/her most connected to you and expand on those.

- Create family rituals like bedtime reading, mealtime discussions, vacations, celebrations, etc. These rituals are the "glue" of the family. You are teaching your child that loving relationships with those close to them feel good and are fun. You are helping them expand from their natural focus on "**Me**" to "**We**."

Connect to Communicate

When your child is coming unglued in the midst of a seemingly unreasonable, illogical outburst, they are functioning within their reactive primitive brain that has formed an unholy alliance with the emotional right brain. **You must connect to the logical left brain before attempting reasonable communication.** You would not direct an attacking mountain lion to "Sit down and stop making all that noise!" or try to reason with her, "Really, I'm old and tough and not at all tasty." That primitive lion brain is not open to suggestion, persuasion or direction no matter how loud, emphatic, right or logical your demand!

If you do try to meet your child's hyper-emotional state with logic, extreme calm, or argument, demands, defense, even your own anger, no matter how sensible or impressive it seems to you in the moment, the result *will be* resentment, more anger and an escalating situation that ends in someone losing a power struggle. Instead, start by *listening*.

Active Listening

The simplest and most powerful word to remember in the realm of communication and connection is **listen.** Even when the words flying at you are ridiculous, flat out wrong, delivered at ear splitting volume, or exquisitely calculated to incite you, *listen*, with undivided attention. Make eye contact and reflect back what you heard. Offer silence, then listen some more. Listening and acknowledging feelings are the most effective techniques you can use to derail an oncoming confrontation freight train and achieve connection.

> *"The best thing that I try to do for myself is to try to listen to the horse - figure out what he understands or what he doesn't understand, what's bothering him and what isn't bothering him. I don't mean let him take over. Try to feel what the horse is feeling and operate from where the horse is."*

Listen with your eyes, ears and heart. Be eager to hear, open to learning, ready to be astonished. Listen without defensiveness, arguing, interrupting the flow or giving advice. Hear about life from your child's perspective. You may learn something new while demonstrating *how* to listen.

Listening and clearly showing that you heard doesn't necessarily mean you agree, it means you understood what was being expressed. Often, (not always) the perception of empathy, the feeling that someone actually understands her feelings is enough to defuse or redirect a difficult situation.

Listening is the first step toward your child hearing *you*.

When she feels heard, the door to the thinking brain creaks open, allowing you to connect using "Connectalk" to guide her towards reason, logical thought and true communication.

Positive or negative, behavior is *always* an attempt to communicate. It's your job to interpret the behavior and help your child translate the emotions into words. Emotions with a name are easier to handle. Show your child that you will *always* seek first to understand and you'll build connection, trust and a sense of safety.

The biggest communication problem is we do not listen to understand, we listen to reply.

Ground Work 5 –Listen With Your Toes!

- With a partner, choose one person (A) who will share a meaningful personal story and describe how it made him/her feel. Person A should talk for about three minutes.

- Person B must *listen so he/she feels the emotion being expressed all the way to his/her toes! No interrupting* at all! Non-verbal expressions of understanding are beneficial and allowed.

- When person A is finished, person B will repeat back what was shared, as completely as possible, including how person A felt about the event.

- Person A will then share how it felt to first be listened to and second to be understood.

- Reverse roles and repeat the sequence.

Connectalk

Connectalk
- It's OK to be sad.
- I can see you're really angry.
- Tell me about it.
- This is hard for you.
- I hear you.
- That was really scary/frustrating disappointing/upsetting/sad.
- I'll help you work it out.
- I'm listening.
- It doesn't feel fair.
- I'll be here when you're ready to talk.
- Oh, that hurt!
- Do you want a hug?

Once you have listened to your child's emotions, use Connectalk to show that you heard. Start the habit of using Connectalk prior to attempting logical communication even before your child is verbal. The younger your child is, the more connection can be facilitated through empathy and labeling emotions, "You are so excited to play with the puppy!" "You sound really angry with Henry." "It makes you sad when grandma leaves." Meet her where she is in her right brain to gain access to the left - without matching out of control emotions.

You do not do this so you can tell them what they should be feeling! You do it to accomplish four vital steps in improving communication:

1. You will assure that you got it right.
2. Your child will feel heard and that you *get it*.
3. Your child will learn the language of emotions and the process of knowing what to do with them.
4. Your child will learn how to listen.

Caution! Do not use special treats or promises to get a child to calm and connect. These become a reward for negative behavior!

Only after you have connected emotionally, can you have any hope of linking the ear holes with the thinking brain!

An extremely disappointed four year old Bertha cried, "I hate Daddy! He said he would take me to the dinner and now he's not gonna! He's just mean and doesn't care about me."

> **Listening and acknowledging feelings are the most effective techniques you can use to achieve connection.**

Mom listened, then said, "You're really angry and disappointed that Daddy can't go with you."

Bertha wailed, "And I hope his plane crashes. I hate him!" This is where it would have been *really* tempting for Mom to react, "You don't mean that, you love your daddy!" But instead...

Mom recognized her own outraged reaction, took a breath and slowly let it out. Then she leaned a bit deeper into Bertha's emotional world, further interpreting her feelings by saying emphatically, "You're really angry that Daddy had to leave, and maybe sad, too?" Lower lip out an inflated inch, Bertha nodded hard enough to dislodge her tiara. Hello left brain.

Mom then asked, "How could you let him know how disappointed you are? Should we write him a note or send a text? Let's write down some ideas for what you could say about how you feel."

In this scenario, Mom listened, connected and moved into the realm of communication without disagreeing or admonishing Bertha for her mean words. Instead she clearly showed understanding of Bertha's feelings until she connected to her thinking brain. She offered her some acceptable outlets for her anger and frustration. Based on Mom's knowledge of what works for Bertha, she could have offered to let her cry, invite her to write, draw, hit a bop bag, kick a box...be her rock while she vents. Then, once the door was open, Mom could move her toward more logical thinking with comments that explored the fact that she is hurt because she loves her daddy so much. Emotional control and connection to the left brain by whatever means works must happen before any attempt at discussion will see success.

One reaction guaranteed to block connection and plunge a knife deep in the relationship is to use comebacks such as, "You don't mean that!" "There's no reason to be so angry," or "It can't be that bad, stop crying." The quip that's always been *guaranteed* to set me off is, "Calm down." Oh, the blue streak of come-backs I've spouted after being told to calm down! *Never* has it helped me calm down – or connect to the person who said it.

If you can't get it together enough in the moment to acknowledge or reflect back feelings, even a simple "Hmmm" will do. "Ahhh," is infinitely better than the classic and dismissive, "It'll seem better tomorrow," or worse, "Let me tell you about real hurt!" These kinds of comments only add the fuel of resentment to a pot already boiling with negative emotions.

That is not to say that you can't ever share a story that demonstrates empathy or helps to put events in perspective. I remember when I was a teen, a friend of my mother's would share stories of her life in a way that helped me understand that "this too, shall pass." When timed and presented well (after listening and without interrupting), personal stories that illustrate your understanding and even add a dose of humor, can build connection. Stories can promote the revelation that the adults in one's life are caring humans that were once young and *can* understand.

Here is an example of how Connectalk might work in the adult world. Imagine you've just come home from a particularly rough day at work and you pour that glass of wine you've envisioned the whole traffic clogged drive home. You share with your spouse, "Our director was so demeaning in the staff meeting today; he berated me for my project being late in front of everyone!"

Spouse #1 says, "I don't know why you don't call him on his crap instead of just taking it." (Straight to fixing the problem with logic.)

Spouse #2 says, "That has to be so frustrating – and embarrassing! I wonder if there's a way to get him to understand how he's making you and everyone else feel?" (A simple statement of understanding, followed by a question.)

What is your gut reaction to each spouse? In what direction will each conversation head? Which spouse would make you feel like he/she is a safe haven where you can share your feelings and frustrations and be heard? Which spouse is more likely to experience a "close" evening later? Practice replacing your initial reactive responses with Connectalk phrases in order to build relationships at home and elsewhere. Be Spouse #2.

When refereeing disputes between children, the first step is as always, to listen, then identify and label the wants and feelings of all involved parties. This lays the groundwork for building the skill of perspective taking which leads to cooperative problem solving. Instead of saying, "You both need to share," try explaining, "You guys sound really upset. Clarita wants the doll and Josie wants to play with the doll, too. What can we do?" With this simple statement and question you have listened and connected to both kids, modeled perspective taking and nudged the combatants toward problem solving.

As soon as he is old enough to understand, ask your child how he thinks

The ability to take the perspective of another is a skill that needs intentional support to develop.

others feel in disagreements, whether he was involved or not. Ask during television shows. The critical ability to take the perspective of another is a skill that needs intentional support to develop and will reap the rewards of connected and fulfilling future relationships.

Consistently adopting an attitude that shows you are in control of your own emotions and that you are there to listen and understand, will promote your children's ability to be aware and in control of their own emotions. You'll build the link to their thinking brain – and to you.

Find the Rhythm

Horseman Richard Winters stresses using rhythm to connect and to sooth rough emotions with horses. With kids, this doesn't mean breaking into the Whip/Nae Nae (though the sight of you rockin' out might take advantage of the laugh track to get from the right to the left brain!), it means getting in tune with the rhythm of your child's emotions. If you meet your child's out of control emotions with a too soft and sweet, "I know honey, you feel really upset right now," you may just get a glare, detachment and more rage for your trouble. Your well-meaning attempts at empathy and understanding may be perceived as condescending and inspire a resentful, "I'll show you upset!" and/or, "You just don't get it!"

Try to meet him just a bit below his level of emotionality, picking up his rhythm, in order to open the door to connection, then guide the level down. An emphatic, "Wow, I can see that *really* made you angry!" or, I bet you did want to hit him back!" will show you really get it and that you're not just trying to placate.

This is a favorite analogy that my trainer Anita uses in riding lessons. Imagine you are in a three legged sack race with your horse (child). You want to get to the finish line first, but you both have one leg in that sack. If you just direct the action without considering the needs and rhythm of your partner, you'll both likely end up spitting dust. The winners of that race work together as a team. You could probably even hear them counting together or saying, "Inside, outside, inside, outside."

When you adjust to your child's rhythm, connection will follow. She will learn to trust your authenticity as well as to listen to the communication rhythms of others.

Get Specific

Review your observations from Ground Work 2 (Page 52) for clues to specific strategies you can use to calm and connect to your child in those out of control moments. Should you calmly wait, get on her eye level, touch, hug, sing, make her laugh? Every child is different; experiment, get specific in finding out what works for yours.

Fred is comforted by a hug when he's upset, but hugs cause Albert to recoil and get angrier. Albert's parent might need to provide an acceptable outlet for his anger, possibly punching a bag or pillow, tearing paper, etc., utilizing his emotional right brain to connect to the logical left. Gertrude may be redirected or distracted by a favorite toy or book, but Wynona escalates with any interaction, especially touch. Her parent might stay quietly nearby and wait, offering a comforting, safe presence, or emphatically name her feelings to open a path to reason. Observe, be flexible and connect according to your child's temperament and timeline. Respond with individual temperament in mind and you'll teach your child that you are a safe outlet for feelings and that connecting to you leads to comfort and resolution.

If you skip the connecting step, the result will be authoritarian parenting and its resulting negative personality traits – resentful, anxious, unhappy, low self-esteem and self-reliance, defiant, and angry; nothing on your list of desirable characteristics.

Get Ahead of it!

Experienced horsemen can be heard saying to students, "Get ahead of it – you're late!" (I hear that a lot.) Recognize the behavior bomb early and defuse it in order to avoid the need to pick up the pieces after the explosion. As soon as your child's brain takes that first slippery step toward an emotional meltdown, he needs your support to help him choose a different path. It's all about timing.

> **Recognize the behavior bomb early and defuse it in order to avoid the need to pick up the pieces after the explosion.**

Name his scary emotions, put events in perspective and help him to see options *before* he reaches the out of control stage. Once any child, but especially an adolescent, becomes angry or defensive, it is too late for reason. The Connect, Communicate and Co-operate cycle will help bring him back. Using the pattern of a statement of understanding followed by a question, "You seem to be getting frustrated (or angry, or scared, or...), do you want to try it a different way or stop and come back later?" will help him become mindful of his own reactions and escalating emotions. Then he can begin to think and be aware that there may be a response choice that doesn't include back-talking, yelling, throwing, hitting, tantruming or other unproductive behavior.

No one wants to deal with a drama queen or king. When you catch escalating emotions early and respond with self-control and empathy, you can reduce your child's need to over-dramatize in order to get your attention. You will teach that her own and others feelings can be understood and respected without exaggerating them. When you model empathy, self-control and problem solving, you lay the foundation for long term positive, reciprocal patterns of communication.

Avoid the Power Struggle

When my younger son Tyler was in kindergarten, his teacher, Mrs. Shepard (name is changed) was having the class participate in a musical number for the spring fling. Her requirement was that *all* the children take part in the singing. This was not a well thought out request to begin with, but add to that, she was dealing with Tyler, who, in Mrs. Shepard's defense, provided my most difficult year of teaching, ever, when he was in my class. It is rarely a good idea to have your own child in your classroom, but add to that, he was a spirited, head strong boy who regularly taught me the value of listening and building connection. She'd had him in class since September, and I would have thought she'd

> *"Do not get in a fight or battle of wills with a horse. It takes two to fight. Take a deep breath, relax and think of a step by step solution to the problem."*

have learned into how best to gain his cooperation. Predictably (key concept), Tyler refused to stand up and sing with the other children. Mrs. Shepard immediately directed him to sit in the time-out chair until he could come join the group in its happy springtime song.

This was forty-five minutes into a two and a half hour class. I picked him up at the end of class, still sitting in the chair. Tyler had won. He had a flat butt and a frown etched on his forehead, but he'd won. Of Mrs. Shepard's several mistakes, a few were:

♡ She didn't **consider** developmentally appropriate goals, her knowledge of herself or of the five year old children in her class (including Tyler) in order to predict reactions, plan her approach or logical consequences.

♡ She made no attempt to listen or to **connect**.

♡ Her **communication** consisted of a directive, without acknowledgement of feelings or questioning.

♡ **Co-operation** was nowhere on the radar – except that she expected it from the students.

♡ She was possibly **consistent**, but not in a good way.

The result: she turned a poorly conceived punishment into an all-out power struggle. The minute she turned the situation into a win/lose battle of wills, she'd lost the battle. And, she made a very unhappy mother in the process.

Those relationship damaging, unproductive power struggles can be avoided by utilizing the Five Mighty C's. When you connect, *then* communicate, an impending battle may be diffused by simply expressing understanding of the other person's feelings. You can then both approach the problem from the same side, working toward a common goal. Battle mode can become unnecessary.

In this example, Mrs. Shepard might have connected by listening, then reflecting Tyler's feelings, "You really don't want to stand up and sing? I know it can be scary." Then, if Tyler was at least making eye contact, "I do need everyone to participate in the pageant (her thought out goal), so would you like to help paint the backdrop or decorate the bridge instead of singing?" This would have shown Tyler that Mrs. Shepard had considered his (and other's) possible objection and was prepared with an alternate plan. Had she demonstrated this bit of compassion for Tyler's feelings, his brain may have inched toward thinking mode and he may have been able to see Mrs. Shepard as a partner, who was attempting to support him; he may have been able to make a choice about alternatives and cooperated in the process, possibly even in the singing. He may have been able to see himself as someone who can make good choices.

> **When the adult listens, then defines the problem and engages the child in solving it, collaboration, cooperation and a stronger relationship are the result.**

When the adult listens, then engages the child in defining the problem and exploring solutions, collaboration, cooperation and a stronger relationship are the result. Mrs. Shepard's authority and control of the situation could have stayed intact.

After the actual incident, can you imagine Tyler's probable feelings toward Mrs. Shepard or toward school in general? What did he learn? What could have been his take-away lessons if Ms. Shephard *had* used the Five Mighty C's?

The Five Mighty C's apply to adult interactions, too. I had to consider my real goal in this situation, which was for Mrs. Sheppard to gain some positive classroom management skills. In order to get there, I had to put my irate Momma Bear self in her den and consider a productive approach. I considered that she would be embarrassed and frustrated. When I put aside my anger and acknowledged her feelings, she was able to trust that we shared a common goal, and we were able to explore some alternatives together.

Caution! Don't be so fearful of saying the wrong thing and damaging the relationship that you analyze an active situation to death before you respond. The time for contemplation is before a "moment." Some situations demand action. If your child is about to hit another child over the head with a block, go grab the block! Firmly state the rule one time, "We do not hurt people!" and take immediate action (remove him from the area). Discussion can wait. The Five Mighty C's can come back into play once there is no danger of injury.

On Boredom

Spending quality time with your child and building the relationship does not mean you are responsible for filling every moment of their lives with fantasticness! Children should have empty time in their day when they have nothing (and *nothing* means no electronics of any kind!) to do, so they can experience the creativity inspired by having to entertain themselves.

When I heard, "I'm boooored!" from my boys, I used to rattle off a list of chores that needed to be done! Not exactly what they were looking for.

Let your child take responsibility for his own boredom. Unless his room looks like a micro-chip manufacturer's sterile room, you are not responsible for your child's lack of "something to do." As long as there is paper, crayons, blankets, dirt, blocks and other "loose parts" around, little Titus can exercise his creative problem solving skills and think of something. Your ability to extricate yourself from chunks of his time will facilitate self-reliance and an appreciation of independent play and creativity. He can learn to know and depend on himself.

Grounded in the knowledge that it is not your responsibility to entertain, you can emphatize, "You can't think of anything you want to do?" Then, turn the responsibility back to her with a question, "What's something you haven't done in a while?" *Do not* get caught in the never ending spiral of making suggestions that will be met with a "Noooo!" A little silence on your part can inspire resoursefullness on her part. Boredom can be a positive motivator.

Research has shown that boredom is a primary reason teens experiment with alcohol, drugs, sex and other detrimental pastimes. Give your kids the opportunity to learn to fill their time with creative, positive, safe diversions while they are young.

"*Communication* is two or more individuals sharing and understanding an idea. If you're both "shouting" at each other you are not communicating. In order to listen to horses, you have to learn how to read them, how to play with them, how to observe their behavior and expressions. You also have to allow them to express themselves. You must be simple and clear in your expressions and expectations."

CHAPTER 5

PRINCIPLE 3, COMMUNICATE

"That's why they call it riding, not sitting. You need to pay attention, interact."

USE THE REINS TO SHARE INFORMATION

Mindful Communication

In *Fully Present, the Science, Art and Practice of Mindfulness*, the authors Sue Smalley PhD and Diana Winston define mindfulness as, "Attention to the present experience with a curious and neutral stance." *Take the Reins!* asks you to bringing this mindful attention to *every* interaction and behavioral challenge in order to enhance your awareness:

♡ Of your own "in the moment" emotions

♡ Of your child's emotions

♡ That this *is* a teachable moment

Developing awareness of these three things in the midst of a heated moment takes practice and amazing self-control, but becoming more mindful of your own emotions *can* help you change your reactions into deliberate and productive responses. You can proceed with your mind wrapped around the goal of creating a stronger **"We."** *We* are going to come out of this situation learning something positive and protecting our relationship.

"You have to not be emotional and not lose your temper. Your horse mirrors your emotions, so when you feel frustrated, your horse is feeling the same thing. Some horses learn that all they have to do is challenge you a little so that you get emotional and loose it and then they can do anything they want. Learn to ride through problems, not lock up on the reins."

Only when you have worked through the three steps listed in Chapter 3, "Consider," and have defined your goals and explored the wonders of you and your child, are you fully equipped to meet your child where he is emotionally.

Successful implementation of the horsemanship rule that **high emotion has no place in discipline** is built on "a curious and neutral stance." Mindful awareness opens the door to emotional control. It is understood that this is a very tall order that includes some serious reining in of emotional reactions!

Rein it In!

Thousands of years of evolution have successfully prepared our reptile brains to handle moments of high emotion with fight, flight or freeze. Adrenalin and other stress hormones flow through our system; blood is pumped away from the higher level reasoning portions of our brain toward our extremities at the very moment when that organ could be most useful! We enter intense conversations and confrontations with our primitive brains on full alert and often fall into some form of resentful silence, sarcasm, defensiveness, or anger and explosion, resulting in reptile brain vs reptile brain. We should not be surprised when we get primitive outcomes!

"There are only two emotions that belong in the saddle. One is a sense of humor and the other is patience."

If your child taps into your reptile brain, causing you to lose it, they've got you! "Wow, look at dad's red face and spittle flying! Dang, I'm good!" **When you lose control, they gain control.** You've just presented your child with a tool to get your goat and you can bet whatever that particular strategy was will be repeated!

When teenage Miss Penelope treats you to that infuriating eye roll and you respond with a tirade, *she's* got control. Instead of giving in to the primitive urge, take a deep breath, note your own inner reactions, connect to your own thinking brain and use these two steps that you've heard mentioned previously:

1. **A calm statement of facts**, "Penelope, you're rolling your eyes."
2. **A simple question,** "Does that mean you think my decision is unreasonable?" (Other questions might include the basics, how, why, what, when, who, etc.)

With those two simple steps you've removed the wind from her antagonist sails. You've shown her that it's just not that easy to push your buttons and get you to lose control. In the process you've taught how to respond and not react. Make this two-step response your new mantra when you're faced with trigger behaviors and you will affirm that you are in charge and cannot be shaken or distracted from your intent. Keep your cool and keep your plan.

Younger children or those with more timid temperaments may not be bold or strong enough to go down a devious "Gotcha!" or "I'm in control" thought path, but may instead become fearful. A show of anger may put a lid on a trigger behavior, but unintentional and resentful lessons may continue to boil inside such as: "I am controlled by other's anger." "I am helpless." "I am bad." "This adult is to be feared." "I hate you." "This is what relationships should look like." Not what you want to teach!

A parent cannot be intentional in their interactions if they are multitasking, feeling overwhelmed, or stressed. Slow life down. When that trigger behavior is offered up, in order to be able to listen and use Connectalk, use a calming technique on yourself, repeatedly if necessary, to access *your* thinking brain. Some calming techniques could include, but are definitely not limited to:

♡ Breathe in, take inventory of your emotions with that "curious and neutral stance" and breathe out.

♡ Remind yourself that this is *normal* testing behavior and not a personal attack.

♡ Remember you are always teaching and recognize that this is an opportunity to be intentional in that teaching.

♡ Use the second Mighty C – *Connect*. Take advantage of that pause when you identify and verbalize your child's emotions to shift your focus away from your anger and toward purposeful communication.

♡ Take a deep breath and release slowly from your gut while feeling your self grounded to the earth.

♡ Choose a calming word or phrase that helps you – "relax," "take it easy," and repeat.

♡ Use visualization. Picture your favorite serene scene and see it, smell it, feel it. Saturate your brain with it.

♡ Ask yourself what getting angry will do and won't do. It won't improve the situation and will teach some of those ugly lessons mentioned earlier.

Great parenting happens when you start controlling yourself and stop controlling your child.

fb.com/humanrightsforhumanchildren

♡ If necessary, step away, do something physical, walk, run, stretch, do yoga, ride your horse, just get some fresh air and a change of scenery. Pick up the conversation again when you can communicate with intention.

Practice your personal calming techniques, and they will become new patterns in your brain that will eventually be your natural, comfortable "way of going."

When the roiling sea of emotions has calmed and there are two integrated, thinking brains present, use "I" statements to discuss your feelings and share what it took to calm yourself. Say, "I was upset that you left the dishes in the sink," instead of, "You never do your chores!" Consider the self-awareness and problem solving skills your child can learn when, instead of reacting with anger, you calm yourself, listen to their point of view, calmly present yours without attacking, and direct their thinking toward solutions. Your child's lesson can become, "I can control *my* emotions." "This is how to handle my anger." "This is how relationships work." "This adult can be trusted to help me, I am safe."

Ground Work 6 – Get Grounded

- List three of your child's behaviors most likely to trigger your frustration.
- List two calming or "grounding" strategies you might use for yourself when those behaviors happen, e.g., take a deep breath, count to ten, visualize a peaceful scene, walk away briefly, get some tape and use it on your mouth. What really works for you?
- Write down the actions and words you would use *after* using your calming technique.
- Practice with a partner. Sounds a bit silly, but if you actually say the words out loud and go through the (e)motions, it will be much easier to do when you really need it. Choose a partner who will be a good actor, able to demonstrate volatile behavior, so you get a true feel for your own reactions.
- Start using your techniques with your children!

Women, choose a moment when you're feeling particularly open to introspection and consider how this excerpt from an article by horsewoman Kathleen Lindley Beckham applies to parenting:

"Women tend to use very little pressure until use of pressure is driven by some emotion like fear, frustration or anger. In our horse work, this is a cardinal sin, and it seems like we're just set up for it. It's a battle to change it. Think of the mother in a parking lot whose kid runs out in front of a car - her passionate scolding (and perhaps punishment) of that child is driven by fear, not by logic or rational planning and thought. Same with our horses. A lot of women will go along with a horse, using very little pressure, letting things slide and become inconsistent, right until some emotion is triggered. Then watch out!!! Lots of pressure and lots of emotion!

Horses don't operate well that way. Horses need to know that things are going to be fair. I think they're way more concerned about fairness than they are about gentleness. So when a woman goes from a bit of pressure to crazed out emotional banshee, it doesn't make any sense to him and he's going to lose confidence and understanding."

You're not a robot and everyone feels anger at times. It's OK to show a little *appropriate* anger as long as you're in control of your emotions enough to use the opportunity to intentionally teach how to express anger and disappointment in an acceptable, non-relationship damaging way. With careful intent, you can use your emotion to connect to your child's emotional brain.

"I understand that you're angry, because right now I'm angry, too! Do you want to talk now or wait till we're both cooled down a bit?"

Praise Vs Acknowledgement - Notice the *Try!*
Develop Growth Mindset and Grit!

> *"If you're busy fighting, you'll never feel the try. The try can be a little thing and you have to have quiet to find his or her idea of a try.*

Dr. Angela Duckworth said, "Grit is passion and perseverance for very long term goals. Grit is having stamina, sticking with your future, working really hard, day in, day out to make that future a reality." Her research, starting in 2005, found the characteristics of grit to be better predictors of staying in school than I.Q. or economic status of the family. How do you develop grit? The most effective way is through **"growth mindset."**

Growth mindset begins with using *acknowledgement, not praise.* There is a big difference between the two in both delivery and long term outcome. Praise is evaluative and often includes the phrase, "I like...," or "Good job," and words such as pretty, handsome, smart, and talented. Praise focuses a child's attention toward outward approval. Acknowledgement is descriptive, specific and focuses on *process or effort*s, letting a child know that they are capable learners.

> *"The wrong kinds of praise can lead kids down the path of entitlement, dependence and fragility."*
> -Dr. Carol Dweck

In her groundbreaking book, *Mindset, the New Psychology of Success,* Dr. Carol Dweck cites evidence that even IQ scores can be negatively impacted by positive labeling. "The wrong kinds of praise can lead kids down the path of entitlement, dependence and fragility." It is best for the developing psyche to catch a child as often as possible doing, attempting to do, even thinking about doing something right and describe what you have noticed; "You took your plate to the sink, thanks." "You knew more answers this time than last, look how much you learned!" "You tried different ways of solving that problem until you finally got it." Efforts that end in failure can become growth moments with comments such as, "You really put in a lot of effort on that piece. What do you think you need to do differently next time?" (*Never* use the sarcastic old standby, "What were you thinking?")

Recognize effort and use observational statements. The first step toward using positive and effective acknowledgement is to **notice the try**. *Notice* that Tucker helped his brother pour milk in his cereal before addressing the puddle of milk next to the bowl. *Notice* Delphinia hung up her discarded clothes, not that her socks don't match. *Notice* Abner brought in a squash from the garden for dinner, not the muddy foot-prints that followed him in. I don't mean to not address the negative, just notice and acknowledge the positive, then address the other stuff. "Thank you for pouring your brother's milk! Here's the sponge for the table." "Thanks, sweetie, we'll have a healthy vegie for dinner tonight. Here, let's use some paper towels to get these footprints cleaned up." You will be amazed at the cooperative spirit you can build. You will see more of the behaviors that you notice and acknowledge.

"Be more positive than negative. We don't notice near enough of the good things he does, and while he's doing those good things, we just take them for granted."

Evaluative phrases like, "Good job," "You are such a good artist," "You are so smart!" become meaningless when overused or not connected to a description of the reason for the praise and they can actually *harm* motivation and performance. Dweck's research shows that children praised in a way that judges (even positively) their *innate* intelligence, talents or looks, do enjoy and appear to benefit from the statements in the moment. However, the minute they run up against a problem, their confidence is lost and motivation disappears. This is due to the fact that over time they form a mindset that makes them less likely to try new things, admit errors or learn from mistakes. The message becomes, "Success means I am smart and failure means I'm dumb so, I won't tackle this difficult problem, because I might fail and be seen as dumb." In this way of perceiving one's self, imperfections are shameful.

> *A side-effect to catching and acknowledging your child's positive behavior is that you will develop more positive feelings about who your child is.*
> -Dr. Wendy McCord

When you reward the try by acknowledging your child's *effort*, you are supporting the thinking process that says, "If I work hard and persevere, I can tackle anything. I can learn from my mistakes. Challenges are fun." Research by Dr. Ng at the University of Illinois comparing Chinese and American families in a controlled IQ test setting in both Illinois and in Hong Kong, showed that Chinese families tended to view achievements as a matter of persistence and plain hard work rather than innate gifts.

Mistakes, errors and confusion are seen as a natural part of the learning process and, most importantly, parents discuss the mistake or failure with their children, coaching them in finding ways to improve.

The American parents were more likely to ignore their children's mistakes and focus only on the positive, seemingly out of the fear that discussing them will damage their child's self-esteem. They appeared to function on the assumption that mathematical or other abilities are innate and "If you have it, you don't have to work hard. If you don't have it, there's no point in trying or addressing the issue."

Your supportive response to errors can help your children learn to use mistakes as steps toward learning. In order to promote creativity, kids must be willing to risk getting the wrong answer, to continue to experiment and learn to discover solutions!

Instead of, "Good Job," get specific, try saying:

- You tried your hardest to _____.
- You prepared well for _____.
- You really improved on _____.
- That was a very responsible/caring /thoughtful thing to do.
- You handled that situation well because you _____.
- I know Claudia appreciated that you _____.
- I can tell you studied hard.
- What a creative way to solve that problem!
- You cleaned up without being reminded!
- _____ was a good choice.
- You remembered to _____.
- You didn't give up, you kept trying different ideas and you did it!
- Can you think of another way to solve it?
- It seemed you took time to consider Penelope's feelings.
- Thank you for _____.

Dweck and others have found that frequently praised children grow more competetive and more interested in tearing others down. Image maintenance becomes their primary concern. If your child is expressing excitement over a good grade or other success, be happy for and with her *and* ask questions that encourage reflection on the effort that was applied. "Congratulations! You won! Did you guys try something new or different this game?"

> **Children must learn to not fear failure, but to view mistakes as steps toward learning.**

Innate talents and natural appearance are not something a child has control over. Praise for appearance is especially detrimental to little girls. (I won't even start on what I think of child beauty pageants!) It's what children *do with* their talents and abilities and how hard they work to learn and contribute that should be applauded. Try to describe how you feel about what they have done without constantly saying, "I like...," to avoid over-dependence on approval. Use phrases like, "Your room is so organized now! You'll be able to find your stuff in a snap!" "You worked hard on that." "That was thoughtful." Focus your words on the behavior, not on the child.

Simple statements spoken from the heart and specifically related to children's actions are most effective. Giving positive attention to the try will teach them that skills and achievement come through commitment and effort. This is the secret to building *self-respect*.

You will see more of the behaviors you give attention to, even if it is negative attention.

Kids crave attention and if their attention bucket is not filled with the positive stuff, *negative attention will do!* They can be very persistent and creative when attention seeking. You do *not* want those formidable skills focused on negative behaviors! Fill their bucket with shared good times: play, work, sing, laugh, walk, cuddle, paint, build, create routines and traditions, get outside, ask their opinion, discuss, debate, listen, and be truly engaged. Give them no reason to need to fill that bucket with the bad stuff! Quiet yourself so you can limit your reactions to negative behavior and acknowledge the good. The horsemen say, "Find the try," then give *it* your attention.

Ground Work 7 – Acknowledgement Vs Praise

First, jot down all the phrases and words you can think of that you normally use to praise your child.

- Then, one evening after your child goes to bed, list five things he/she did that day deserving of your usual praise.
- List as many descriptive statements that recognize effort ("I see that you really worked hard to _____." "Thanks for cleaning up _____.") as you can think of that might have been appropriate to use.
- Practice: Start with the goal of using two phrases of acknowledgement for effort per day, for one week. The next week, increase it to three, then to four per day, etc.
- Notice if your child's negative behaviors decrease as your positive attention and authentic acknowledgement of positive behavior increases.

Caution! - Research confirms that criticism is much more impactful on the brain than praise. Even inappropriate or empty praise is better than criticism. When perceiving negative words, the brain focuses on nothing else. This becomes all-consuming and the effect can be lasting. Visualize your child sitting in a row boat on the ocean. Every criticism, put down, or sarcastic comment blows a hole in the boat. These are remembered when your child considers his own value. Every shared moment of closeness or joy, every acknowledgement and bit of understanding, every smile, touch or hug increases the size and strength of the boat. Build them a cruise ship!

Kidwhispering – The "best of" experience-based kid communication strategies

Talk *with* your children at non-fractious, comfortable moments as well as when directing, correcting, investigating or planning, etc. Ask questions that:

- ♡ **Draw out and show genuine interest** in their thoughts and opinions. "Do you think he did the right thing? Why? What would you have done?"
- ♡ **Are open-ended** – Ask for specifics so your question is not answerable with a conversation ending "Yes," "No" or "Fine."
- ♡ **Are age appropriate** - Never ask a very young child questions like, "Why did you do that?!" He may truly have no idea and couldn't explain it if he did.
- ♡ **Clarifying** – "Tell me what happened." "How do you think she felt when you did that?"
- ♡ **Thought provoking** - "What would happen if...?"
- ♡ **Problem solving** - "If Josh takes the car away from you again, what could you do?"

Bravely discuss loaded or uncomfortable topics such as race, lying, death, religious beliefs, substance abuse, sex, relationships, mistakes (theirs and yours), etc. Kids go through critical periods when they are forming opinions on sensitive topics and you need to be ready to discuss them when their curiosity is piqued. This is not usually when you think your child should be ready or when you are prepared with insightful and profound answers! Follow your child's lead and answer from your heart. Address topics when they have opened the door to their thinking brain.

As always, start by listening. You want to answer his actual question and not something you assumed he was asking. If Herbert asks why Alma is different than him, don't launch into a detailed description of girl parts and boy parts and human reproduction when he really wanted to know why Alma has brown skin and he doesn't.

On Lying

Young kids lie for a variety of reasons:
- ♡ It is a simple solution to a problem.
- ♡ They are experimenting with lying.
- ♡ They are using their imagination and fantasizing.
- ♡ To avoid hurting someone's feelings.
- ♡ To avoid punishment – to get away with something.
- ♡ Just for kicks – testing!

When your child is lying, let her know immediately that you know she is lying and stick to established consequences. The more she gets away with it, the more likely it is to continue. Do not use or threaten punishment (they are different, see Punishment vs Consequences, page 124); as it has been shown to actually increase lying. **The most effective thing you can do is emphasize that telling the truth is the right thing to do.** Explain that lying is wrong and that it diminishes trust. Acknowledge and appreciate when they come clean.

Don't set them up to lie by asking if they did something when you already know the answer. Instead of "Did you spill the milk?' ask, "How did this happen?" If you find cigarettes in your teen's room, don't ask if he is smoking, ask, "When did you start?" Don't kick off a difficult discussion by inviting a lie.

Tell the truth yourself – the more they hear lies, the more they'll think lying is normal and acceptable.

Build language and comprehension by narrating what you and they are doing for the young and even what you are thinking for older children. For the very young, describe what is happening to them. "I'm going to take you into day care and say goodbye, then I'll see you again when I pick you up right after nap time." "You were so careful and stacked your blocks sooo high!" Even with newborns, say, "I'm going to pick you up now," "Let's go change that wet diaper" or "I'm washing your back, now your leg." "I love you sooo much!"

I believe in the truth of this quote from Pamela Druckerman in her book, *Bringing up Bebe*, "The French believe that when they speak to a baby, they are not just calming her with the sound of a parents voice; they're conveying important information. They think that explaining things to an upset baby can calm her down." Babies comprehend more than we know.

With older children, when you verbalize your thoughts, they will learn the process of making decisions and setting priorities. "Jan really wants me to help with the fundraiser, but I feel like that will just be too much for me right now. It'll be hard, but I need to say no." These conversations build connection, vocabulary, comprehension, and integrated brains.

Boost language development with responsive interaction. If you are considering using baby DVDs to boost your baby's vocabulary, don't bother. Research by Heart and Wisley at the University of Washington in 2007 revealed that many baby videos can actually have a negative impact on language development. It's believed that the presentation of a disembodied voice over abstract visual images makes no sense to a baby and can even cause confusion. Showing a real person's talking face on the screen makes some difference by allowing sensory integration of voice and visual image, but the most dramatic language development happens with a live human that interacts and *responds* to a baby's utterances and movements. The act and timing of response are what encourages language. Videos don't respond.

Timing is also critical when naming items in your baby's environment. Watch their expression and eye gaze, timing your naming of an item with where their gaze is focused. Engage in face to face, give and take, responsive encounters. Mimic their sounds and attempts at words with your best "Parenteze," a higher pitched voice, emphatic smile, touch and love. The turn taking rhythm of speech interactions helps to develop language as well as strengthen connection. Listen, respond, listen, respond...

"It's not just about shoving words in," said Kathryn Hirsh-Pasek, a professor of psychology at Temple University. *"It's about having these fluid conversations around shared rituals and objects, like pretending to have morning coffee together or using the banana as a phone. That is the stuff from which language is made."*

Teach conversation by extending it. If you want to know how your child's day at school was, ask in a way that can't be answered with one word like, "Fine." Instead, extend the conversation by asking for specifics, "What was the best thing that happened in school today?" "What did you learn new in math?" Don't stop there! Show interest by continuing to ask clarifying questions, "What made recess the best part?" "Who do you like to play with at recess?" "What is the hardest thing to understand about math?" Make, "Tell me more about that" your go-to question. Try for a minimum of three back and forth exchanges every time you converse.

It is amazing how easy it is to fall into giving directives or having only custodial conversations with your children and not actually communicating. Show that you are interested in hearing about your child's life. Teach the pleasure of conversation and how to show genuine interest in another person.

Ground Work 8 – Take Inventory

- Choose a one hour block of time when you will be with your child.
- Make two columns on a small note pad, one titled *Directives* and the other, *Conversations*. Put the note pad in your pocket where it's handy.
- Try to interact as you normally do. Under *Directives*, keep a simple tally of how many times you give your child a direction. "Come eat your breakfast." "Get your coat," "Take the cat out of the toilet." You get the idea.
- In order to count a tally in the *Conversations* column, the exchange needs to include at least one open-ended question and **three** back and forth exchanges.
- Compare the counts of the two columns. How can you improve on these counts?

Encourage your child to expand on her story, especially if she has experienced something upsetting. When she repeats a story related to a distressing incident, she is actually building the portions of the brain that help her deal with traumas, large or small. "This important step calms down the emotional circuitry of the brain and sets the stage for a lifetime ability to cope with difficult situations" (Siegel and Bryson, *The Whole Brain Child*). Ask her to share her story and listen with undivided attention. Let her repeat it as often as necessary – up to a point. I would caution that too much focus on negative incidents over time can over fill that bucket with negative attention, creating a desire for that type of interaction and a negative continuum. Be sure your bucket is balanced with the positive.

Use positive statements whenever possible. Say, "Blocks are for building, balls are for throwing." Not "Don't throw the blocks!" "Sit on the chair, please." Not, "Don't climb on the table!" When your child wants to do something, or to go somewhere but has not completed a request from you or a chore, say, "You can go outside after your homework is done," instead of, "You're not going out till your homework is done." You will focus their thoughts on the positive action that you are asking for while building willing cooperation.

Use the power of "Yet." Add this powerful little word to the sentence when your child says, "I can't!" When you say, "You can't do it *yet*," you move from a focus on the present frustration to opening possibilities for the future. Comments like "You're still learning, you'll get it." project confidence in her ability to learn and grow. Dr. Dweck described how emphasizing the word "yet" helps children see themselves on a learning curve, "Just the words 'yet' or 'not yet,' we're finding, give kids greater confidence, give them a path into the future that creates greater persistence."

A bit o'silence can be just what's needed. At times, just your presence and undivided attention are all that is needed to connect. Carve out a routine that includes quiet, approachable time when your child knows you are there just to listen.

When my boys were young, one quiet time was their bath time. We'd do the washing and some tub play, but I would occasionally ask, "Is there any-thing you want to talk about?" or, "You know you can always tell me anything," followed by silence. This was stated just often enough for them

Listen and Silent are spelled with the same letters.

to know it was "open discussion" time. Once, when my oldest was almost seven and playing in the tub with his little brother, he took me up on this bath time offer and told me something important and very disturbing about a neighbor. Looking back, I hate to think what might have happened if he hadn't shared.

Another great opportunity for quiet communication is bed time. A few quiet moments lying together in the dark can encourage even older children and teens to talk. *LISTEN*. Create a safe atmosphere for sharing feelings without judgment. You may be surprised at what you hear.

Children often need a moment of silence to process their feelings and thoughts on what was just said or asked or what just happened. They need time to find the words to express themselves or figure out the solution to a problem. That shift from reptile brain to thinking brain may need a pause in the action in order to fully engage. Wait a beat after you ask a question to allow for processing time. This will allow him to be successful at handling small chunks of a question or problem before more questions or expectations are added on. This is especially true for kids with disabilities. They often need extra time to gather their thoughts and process a response.

Offering silence instead of solutions can help your child to problem solve, figure out a solution or fix a mistake herself. Let her take responsibility and show that you trust her to handle a problem herself by staying out of it. Experience is the best teacher and it's often most helpful to just stay close, but quiet and let those natural consequences do their job. If she is really stuck, instead of offering solutions, ask "what if" questions that prompt discovery of her own answers. Review her problem solving process with her after the fact in order to acknowledge her efforts and help her learn from any mistakes.

> *"Give the directive one time. Say, 'Whoa' then if he does not stop, use reinforcement. Do not keep repeating, 'Whoa, whoa, whoa,' the words will become meaningless."*

Offer your children opportunities to enjoy comfortable silence. There's no need to fill every moment with empty chatter. Balance is the key. The gift of silence has so many rewards.

Answer once. Say it once. This is huge! If you really want your children to listen to you, once you've responded to a want or complaint, made a request, given a choice, or stated consequences, *do not repeat!*

When your child has made a bad choice, state calmly and clearly what the infraction was and move on to fixing it! Don't dwell, don't repeat, don't turn up the volume. If you've done your relationship building ground work, your perceived disappointment or *brief* flash of anger accompanied by a comment such as, "I'm really disappointed that you chose to _____," will be enough. Later, explore alternatives to his actions and their consequences, together.

The younger the child, the fewer words they can attend to. However, if you turn a request or reprimand into a harangue at any age, repeating what you've asked him to do,

> **The more words you use to make your point, the less meaning those words have.**

his bad choices, or how angry he made you, he will tune you out and you will be teaching him to do just that! Your words become meaningless. (Picture the adult voices in the Charlie Brown cartoons. A muffled, "Wa, wa, wa...")

Discussions around food are always dangerous ground for falling into an unnecessary pit of repetition. If Olivia refuses to eat her dinner, explain the consequences of her choice *one time*. "If you don't eat your dinner, you'll be hungry later." Then, casually pick up her plate when everyone else is done and move on.

Begging is unattractive and diminishes strength. "Come on Olivia, try just one bite. Don't you like chicken nuggets? If you eat your vegies, you can have dessert!" This is a great recipe for creating long term eating problems by putting focus on negative behavior, starting an unwinnable power struggle and teaching Olivia that this is an arena that she *can* control – not good.

Most kids will make fairly healthy food choices and create a lifetime of good eating habits if offered healthy options and food isn't made into a battle ground. They won't starve themselves and meals can be an opportunity to experience positive decision making. It is also logical that if one does not eat one's dinner, one must not be hungry for dessert or snacks later. There will be more food at breakfast time. Give yourself a break and let those natural consequences do their work.

Classic whining usually involves a child asking a question repeatedly. He does this because in the past it has been effective in getting what he wants, or at the very least, in getting his parent to engage and repeat an answer – hopefully until he gets a different answer. Many experts recommend the "Asked and Answered" response. The second time Fritz squeaks out, "But I *want* to ride my skateboard in the street!" his mother does not repeat her original answer, she simply states, "Asked and answered."

I suggest expanding on that strategy by answering the repeated question with a question, "What was my answer the last time you asked?" *This* you repeat as many times as necessary. This response engages your child's thinking and speaking processes instead of putting the responsibility all back on you. He has to think back to what you already answered and say it aloud, answering his own question. He has to acknowledge not only that the question has been asked and answered, but that he heard and understood the answer. He also learns that you can't be sucked into the manipulative, "I will get my way with whining" game!

Offer choices, but only when there really is one. Offering limited choices is a powerful strategy for supporting a child's growing autonomy. Be aware that you are also offering a choice when you end a request with, "OK?" Unless your intent is that he really does not *have* to do whatever it is you are asking, don't turn your request into a question. If you say, "Bruce, I need you to come with Mommy, OK?" you've opened the door to a "No!" answer.

If a trip to the grocery store is inevitable, but the time is open, you could ask, "We need to go to the grocery store today. Do you want to go before lunch or after?" Don't ask "Do you want to go to the grocery store today?" unless you can live with the answer and really are undecided about going.

Body language is powerful. Ninety percent of communication is non-verbal. Consider these two examples of how body language and movement send potent unintentional messages especially when related to leadership.

My friend and fellow horsewoman Jenni, shared an experience that illustrated for her, then for me, that the impact of even subtle body language is as relevant to children as it is horses. We'd been taught that when horses are in pasture with other horses, the horse who causes another to move its feet is considered the leader or higher in the hierarchy. On a recent shopping trip, Jenni had noticed that her ten year old daughter Petunia was being extra clingy and demanding. They were looking at some dresses on a rack for her older sister when Petunia *again* stood very close in front of Jenni, and pushed back just a bit. When Jenni stepped back to see around her, she realized with a little ripple of shock, "She just moved my feet!" Petunia wanted to gain some control, and Jenni gave it to her without saying a word.

Fourteen year old Elmer had ignored a family rule. Dad's good intent when entering Elmer's room was to connect so they could discuss the incident. While dad was leaning against the dresser, Elmer was plopped on the bed with his arms crossed, glaring at the floor no matter what dad said or how he said it. This was not going according to Dad's plan, so he decided to try sitting on the bed next to him and ventured a touch on the shoulder. Elmer turned to face his dad and began to listen and to talk.

It's important to be aware that our bigger bodies looming over a child can be perceived as a controlling or domineering posture. Looming over may achieve conformity, but not connection. Sitting close, facing each other at the same level, making eye contact, locks in a safety zone for communication. Getting down on a young child's level to look him in the eye may not be great on the knees, but is worth the effort if your goal is connection.

Constant attention to electronics sends a clear message about what is important to you. Saying "uh huh" to a toddler or shaking a rattle at your baby with your nose pointed at your phone or the TV does NOT project genuine interest! Kids, like horses are extremely attuned to non-verbal language. We need to be sensitive to the messages they are sending us and aware of the potent non-verbal messages we are sending them.

Be courteous and polite to each other. When you naturally use "Please," and "Thank You," in everyday conversation, there shouldn't be a need to issue an embarrassing and demeaning reminder to say it in front grandpa or the aunties.

Lighten up! Enjoy! Be silly, sing, play, laugh and don't take yourself too seriously.

Never be too busy or distracted to converse! To children, it's all big stuff. Try not to interrupt, argue, lecture or preach, always be ready to listen with 100% of your attention. You'll be happy you took the time to establish this pattern as part of your relationship when your kids become teens and adults.

Hug 'em. Say "I love you."

Use these simple communication strategies and you will improve your and your child's skills in conflict resolution, self-control, understanding, and problem solving, all while supporting connectedness and building your relationship. ***Mindful communication builds confidence from the inside out.***

Ground Work 9– Positive Questioning

Make a list of open-ended, clarifying questions appropriate to your child's age and temperament ("What would happen if...?" "How do you think they felt?"). Include three or more questions that could be used for each of these occasions:

1. **Play time,** to promote creative thinking and problem solving.
2. **After an incident** where he has misbehaved, to promote learning from mistakes and self-control.
3. **When she is emotional**, to promote understanding of her emotions.

Set a goal of using two of these questions per day, and increase the number every few days.

When you're comfortable with asking questions, practice extending the conversation to three, four or more back and forth exchanges.

"How could we make it taller?"

"I dunno."

"What if we used the smaller blue blocks?"

"That might work."

"You wanna put one here or here?"

"I'll stand it up this way."

Don't let directives become your primary mode of communication.

Communication Builders

- *Connect. Listen actively; hear with your eyes, ears and heart.*
- *Acknowledge and clarify feelings.*
- *Rephrase what you heard.*
- *Use specific and clear requests.*
- *Describe the situation with facts, "The toys are all over the floor," instead of, "Pick up your toys!"*
- *Ask appropriate and open-ended questions, "What do you think would happen if...?"*
- *Get on eye level and make eye contact. Touch.*
- *Share your own feelings with "I" statements, "I'm confident in you."*
- *Stay calm, control your own emotions.*
- *Use as few words as possible to make a point.*
- *Write a note.*
- *Offer silence.*
- *Provide acceptable ways to express anger.*
- *Notice and acknowledge effort and positive behavior.*
- *Model respectfulness. Use manners.*
- *Offer acceptable choices.*
- *Problem-solve together. Strive for win/win solutions.*
- *Use respectful humor. Make up a silly song to get tasks like chores, tooth brushing or bed time done.*
- *Ask, "What can I do to help you feel less - afraid, angry, worried?"*
- *Role-play troublesome or uncomfortable scenarios*

Communication Barriers

- *Attacking the <u>person</u>, humiliating, name calling*
- *Denying or dismissing another's feelings, "It can't be all that bad..."*
- *Vague requests, "Henry!" "Behave!"*
- *Interrupting, dominating, threatening intimidating, commanding, yelling, pleading*
- *Moralizing, prophesizing, "You're gonna end up in prison if you keep acting like that!"*
- *Advising, or giving logical arguments prematurely*
- *Lecturing, analyzing, diagnosing*
- *Judging, criticizing, blaming*
- *Playing the martyr, "You're just killing me!"*
- *Sarcasm, teasing, embarrassing*
- *Horrible-izing – taking another's point to an extreme in order to make it sound ridiculous*
- *Threatening, warning, or attacking*
- *Using questions inappropriately, "What is wrong with you?"*
- *Parroting, mimicking*
- *Comparing, "Why can't you be more like your brother?"*
- *Discussing your child in front of him/her.*
- *Dwelling on the past.*
- *Saying anything that starts with "See," as in, "I told you so."*
- *Saying anything that starts with "Don't...worry, cry, be shy, be afraid, be mad."*

"If every time a question is asked, you give the answer, the learner doesn't learn to seek the answer on his own. When you take over the horse's responsibilities instead of teaching him to uphold them, there can be no partnership. It will be something more like master and slave. The human becomes more domineering and less effective and the horse becomes mindless."

CHAPTER 6

PRINCIPLE 4, CO-OPERATE

"If you are going to teach a horse something and have a good relationship, you don't make him learn it – you let him learn it."

MOVE FORWARD TOGETHER

We Win-Win

Co-operation in *Take the Reins!* does *not* mean that the goal is to make your childdren cooperate, as in, "I win – you lose!" It refers to communication, prior to and/or at the close of any incident that conveys the message, *"We win-win."* Co-operation demonstrates that your intent is not, "I control your behavior, and you bend to my will," but, "I'll help you learn to control your own behavior." *We* are in this together, what can *we* do to solve the problem? **"We" is more important than "Me."**

Dr. Tracy Tomasky says in her book *The Conscious and Courageous Leader: Developing Your Authentic Voice to Lead and Inspire,* "Being a conscious leader is about letting go of judgement, criticism and the need to be right." This important principle must be a fundamental part of your identity if you are to be successful in co-operating. Being a conscious leader is taking responsibility for, not power over, others. In parenting, it means guiding your children in their learning, not making them learn.

Family Values, Rules and Routines

An easy and purposeful place to kick off co-operation is defining family rules and their consequences together as a team. Rules not only build family unity, they show kids that you care. Rules allow you to refer back to an agreement that was created using everyone's productive, thinking brains so that during those volatile reptile brain moments you can say, "We agreed that if you didn't pick up your toys before leaving, the toys would be taken away for one week." "We read two books, now it's time to go to sleep." These kinds of simple, unemotional statements of the rules serve to get everyone involved focused on a solution instead of needing to place blame or spark a power struggle where, "I am right and you are wrong," or "You *will* do as I say," is the only possible outcome.

As soon as your children can comprehend respecting the needs of others, have them participate in creating family rules and routines. Their buy-in supports the process of co-operation, and builds the essential sense of "We." It will demonstrate how commitment to family as a priority should work. *We* are a team working together to build a good life for all of us.

When rules, routines and limits are mutually understood and consistently upheld, children feel less need to continually test to find out where their limits are. This doesn't mean they won't find creative new ways to test you; it is their job after all. And the little buggers tend to grow and change, and so does life, creating an ongoing need for them to test newly opened boundaries. Continuing the process of defining and updating family values and rules keeps testing to a minimum and helps you to be confident and consistent in your expectations and responses.

> **When rules, routines and limits are mutually understood and consistently upheld, children feel less need to test to find out where their limits are.**

Children grow happier, more secure and confident when expectations include a few well thought out, age appropriate, consistently enforced limits. Recent research has emphasized that fewer, more general rules help keep creativity alive in children. Kids need to experience the freedom to explore and seek out new experiences, to think for themselves, to try and to fail. Write your rules so they read as family values as much as possible making them general enough to be applicable in a number of situations. They should encourage freedom of expression within your nonnegotiable limits. One of my favorite value/rules that even the youngest children can understand is, "We don't physically or emotionally hurt ourselves or others." It covers a lot of territory, but is simple and clear.

> *"Never do for a child what a child can do for himself."*
> -Rudolph Dreikurs

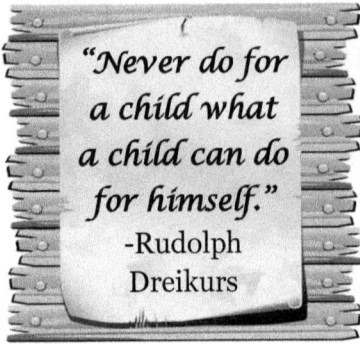

Chores are part of being a family and everyone should be expected to contribute to the family welfare, whether you decide that some, all or none of the chores should have payment attached. Research indicates that children who are responsible for a set of chores have higher self-respect, are more responsible and are better able to deal with frustration and to delay gratification, all of which contribute to greater success in school and life. In fact, says researcher Marty Rossman, "the best predictor of young adults' success in their mid-twenties was that they participated in household tasks from when they were three or four." By doing less *for* kids and expecting more, you create a sense of purpose and belonging while building responsibility. **Offer every opportunity possible for your children to be responsible and feel capable.**

On Chores:

Choose chores that are appropriate for your child's age (but, don't underestimate what they are capable of!) and that you are willing to follow through on enforcing. Some ideas by age group:

2-3	Help cook, garden, make their bed, pick up toys, dust, put laundry in the hamper
4-5	+ Help shop and put away groceries, set the table, sort laundry, care for pets, cook, garden, clean room, make own bag lunch
6-7	+ Make bed, fold laundry, vacuum, dust, empty trash, do dishes and put away, plan and prep meals, keep room clean
8-& Up	+ Homework, yard care, use washer & dryer, wash car, trash to curb, change sheets...

Doctors Nancy Darling and Linda Caldwell at Penn State University did a study of how much teens lie and what they lie about. No big surprise – they lie, avoid talking about, or tell half truths about just about everything. They lie about what they spend their allowance on, dating, clothes worn away from the house, movies, who they are with, alcohol and drugs, how they spend their time, parties, riding in cars driven by intoxicated friends, homework, music, sex and so much more. Ninety-six percent of the teens reported lying to their parents.

Many parents questioned in the study thought that if they were permissive and didn't set rules, their teens would be closer and more open with them. Darling found that permissive parents don't actually learn more about their children's lives. Kids who go wild and get in trouble mostly had parents who didn't set rules or standards, but were loving and accepting no matter what their kids did. Ng found that these kids actually felt that the parent didn't care or didn't really want the job of being a parent. The flip side, parents who set too many rules either didn't enforce them or were overly strict and oppressive. The kids of oppressive (authoritarian) parents may have been more obedient, but they were often also depressed.

The teens that lied the least had parents who set a few rules addressing key areas in life, explained why the rules are important, were consistent in enforcing them and expected their children to obey them. They supported autonomy in other areas of their children's lives and allowed them freedom to make their own decisions. They were warm and had numerous conversations with their children about serious topics. Carefully consider your rules and make them important, realistic and enforceable, but *do* make them.

Make your life easier by creating rules that address problem areas ahead of time. Skirmishes over morning routines, picking up after one's self, safety, household chores, shopping, routines for bedtime, meals, bath, etc. can be reduced with well-considered clarity in expectations.

Create consequences during your family planning sessions. Time spent getting their buy-in will become all important when you come up against the need to enforce the rules. The ability to say, "Remember, we agreed _____," puts you on the same side, working it out as a team. Kids can be amazingly resourceful in arguing their way out of a rule and its consequence. They will test your authority to the max, but you *cannot* give in! A well thought out and written document will provide a strong foundation for your ability to be consistent.

> **Take the Reins! is a framework for interacting and your particular rules of engagement are up to you, however...**

I know I said that *Take the Reins!* is a framework for interacting and your boundaries, your particular rules of engagement are up to you. This is true *and* I'm going to share a few research-based suggestions for you to consider adding to your list of rules.

To help assure optimal positive brain development (see (Zhou 2011, Yuan 2011, Weng 2013, and Weng 2012, page 30), I encourage you to consider a rule regarding screen time - TV, computer, video games, and any hand-held devices. I'm not promoting eliminating them altogether. I believe there is value in in *some* exposure, so their brains are wired to work and think in the ways of modern technology. (I'm acutely aware of this need every time I desperately seek out someone under thirty to help me figure out an issue on my iPhone!) There is little danger any child will not get *enough* screen time. But, in order to reinforce your value of face to face interactions, creative exploration, physical activity, and general family togetherness; in order to create a balanced, highly functional human being, you must limit screen time.

When you do allow TV, try to stay present, discuss what you are watching and use it as a catalyst to build critical thinking skills. Ask questions and listen. Even during commercials you can ask school agers, "What are the advertisers are trying to sell? What are they using to get you to buy it?" Try not to use screen time as babysitter. Don't beat yourself up on the rare occasion that you have to – life happens, just be aware of the effects and keep it to a minimum.

Another rule referring to today's technology is put out by the American Academy of Pediatrics (Guidelines Published in October, 2013). "Children should not be allowed access to cell phones in their bedrooms unsupervised. Put them on a charger in *your* room at night."

Many topics that were viewed as "givens" in the past now need to be defined as family rules because of the wide spectrum of choices and opportunities presented by today's complex and technologically accessible society. For example, it used to be, "just the way it is," that families gathered and ate dinner together. With today's technology options, diverse interests and busyness, even the all-important family dinner (without electronics) has to be defined as a priority if it's going to happen.

In the past, disrespecting parents or other adults was not tolerated. Children wouldn't dare or even consider it! Today, examples of amazingly disrespectful behavior can be seen in schools, in the media and among friends, creating a need for an agreed on rule defining disrespect and its consequences.

Revisit your family rules and the consequences of ignoring them at least annually. It should be a living, well-used and referred-to document. Hang on to your tried and true guiding principles, but tweak the way they are applied. Two year olds may only be able to remember two or three general rules, but school agers definitely need more and teens especially benefit from being a part of the ongoing defining of values and creation of rules. Illustrate an updated poster defining the family rules together and place it where everyone can see it.

Ground Work 10– Family Values & Rules

- With your parenting partner, if appropriate, create a *thorough* list of values and rules that you feel are important and age appropriate for your family. They can be related to interactions with each other, cleaning up and chores, meal and bed time, hygiene, pet care, everything!
- Now shorten that list by half, keeping only the most crucial.
- For each remaining rule and routine, write a natural, logical or imposed consequence for not following it.
- After completing this exercise, create an agreed upon set of rules as a family. Everyone's opinion should be heard! They don't need to be the same rules you came up with, but you will go into the family meeting knowing what is most important to you.
- Make a poster of your family rules together. Decorate it – add pictures, frame it and put it up on the wall for reference.
- Make it a "living document." Go back and revisit whenever necessary. Add and edit rules as family life evolves.
- Be consistent in expectations and enforcement!

When the need arises to enforce the rules, instead of making a request, state the facts and describe the situation in as few words as possible. When you say, "The garbage is full," instead of, "Melvin, please go take out the garbage," Melvin is required to think about what his responsibility is in relation to the full garbage instead of reacting with reflexive opposition to a direct request.

Empathize if it becomes necessary to implement a consequence, "It's frustrating to lose your Legos for a week." Then express confidence that next time he will remember. "I know you'll remember to pick them up before you leave next time."

When Egbert calls asking you to bring him his baseball cleats that were his responsibility to bring to school this morning, in order for natural consequences to do their work, you have to say, "No." Empathize, "I know it's embarrassing to sit out practice or to wear your regular shoes. I'm sure you'll remember tomorrow." Oh, he'll be angry as a hornet, but you let him know that you understand his anger, embarrassment or frustration and express confidence that he can fix the situation. This approach puts focus on the rule and confirms your firm and consistent supporting role, helping him make better choices and take responsibility. The most difficult charge to you as an authoritative parent is to *stick to the consequence.*

Do *not* undermine your own authority by making excuses for not rescuing him. Lifting the parental responsibility off yourself by saying "I just don't have time to bring it to you," devalues your leadership and invites argument. Calmly refer back to the rule or agreement and do not give in to arguing or pleading to be rescued.

If a situation arises where there is no thought out, specific rule to fall back on, you'll need to do more thinking on your feet, which if you're not careful, can lead to ill-considered reactions. When in doubt, *"Connect, Communicate and Co-operate"* to reach a positive outcome.

Three-year-old Geraldine has never thrown a tantrum before, but while on a play date, she threw a doozey (this is an example of a Type 2 tantrum, see page 139) when Bailey kicked down her block structure. Mom took Geraldine aside and asked what happened.

"Bailey knocked down my house!"

Mom, "Oh no! I bet you were really angry when she did that!"

"Bailey's a stupid head!"

Mom, "Screaming, throwing yourself down and kicking are not how we act when we're angry. We are leaving *now*." With apologies to Bailey's mom and a longing farewell glance at her half-drunk mocha, Mom escorts Bailey to the car.

In this scenario, Mom:

♡ **Connected**, by picking up the emotional rhythm and meeting Geraldine in her right brain, "Oh no!" and acknowledging her feelings, "You were really angry!" She *didn't react* by yelling at her to calm down and stop acting like a maniac *or* by saying, "Now Sweetie, its ooohhh...kaayyy..."

♡ **Communicated**, by describing the situation and a general rule, "We do not throw ourselves down and scream and kick when we're angry," and she removed her from the situation as an immediate and logical consequence to her behavior.

💗 Later, she and Geraldine can **Co-operate** by reviewing the incident with two thinking brains. They can explore how Geraldine felt as well as acceptable options for expressing anger and getting help when needed. They can then add to or create a new rule together.

The specifics of the solutions are not as important as the principles used to guide the interactive process of the incident in which Geraldine learned:

💗 That tantrums don't work.

💗 That her behavior was unacceptable and has consequences.

💗 That she can *choose* to behave differently.

💗 That Mom is clearly on her side, and is a safe outlet for her feelings.

💗 That they can reach the mutual goal of Geraldine learning to express anger in acceptable and effective ways.

Mom achieved balance by being a strong and confident leader who mindfully used a behavioral outburst as an opportunity to teach (to discipline) while using empathy to maintain connection.

Now, Mom's job is to avoid hovering, step back and expect positive behavior as she lets Geraldine interact freely. Geraldine then learns to be responsible for handling her own emotions and controlling her own behavior.

"Try not to look for quick fixes with horses. Though they might work temporarily, at the expense of the horse, often the issue is just forced underground, leaving the underlying problem there to grow and fester."

Punishment vs Consequences

"Punishment" does not always fit the crime. It is often a threat, blurted out by a parental reptile brain, that may or may not be followed through on (and if it's not, leadership is weakened). Punishment may force an unwanted behavior to stop through fear and intimidation, but will foster resentment as the child focuses on his anger over the punishment instead of on his own behavior.

Those negative emotions, left to fester, feed an adult win/child lose power struggle. There is no sense of co-operation with punishment. It sends the messages, "You against me," "I win, you lose," and "I control your behavior, you don't." Conversely, when agreed upon consequences are implemented, the focus becomes the child controlling his or her own behavior.

"FOUR R's OF PUNISHMENT
1. Resentment: "This is unfair. I can't trust adults."
2. Revenge: "They're winning now, but I'll get even."
3. Rebellion: "I'll do just the opposite to prove that I don't have to do it their way."
4. Retreat into:
   a. Sneakiness: "I won't get caught next time."
   b. Reduced self-esteem: "I'm a bad person."

Dr. Jane Nelsen, *Positive Time-Out*

Natural consequences are fabulous teachers if you can make yourself let them happen! Its 50 degrees outside and five year old Irene goes out to play without her coat. Mom recognized this as an opportunity and got out a piece of duct tape to use on her

> **Give the gift of silence when your child is about to make a reasonable mistake.**

own mouth. She let Irene experience *appropriate* natural consequences. (Appropriate does *not* mean its okay to let little sweetness run into the street, jump off a bridge or let the dog starve to teach her a lesson!) Irene is simply going to come in later, cold. Hopefully, next time she'll wear the coat. Mom wasn't negligent; she gave her the gift of experiencing natural consequences and figuring out how to solve the problem herself, teaching her responsibility. And all this was accomplished by not saying a word. A follow-up discussion reviewing the sequence of events will cement the lesson.

Mistakes and failures are going to happen when your kids are out in the big bad world by themselves, so allow them to experience them while under your wing so you can be there to help turn them into learning experiences that are not live changing.

> *"Trust that your horse will respond to what you ask but be ready to correct, no more one than the other. Never ask a horse to do something that you are not committed to following through on. If you ask and fail, you have successfully trained your horse to be disobedient. You have to keep up your actions through the undesirable behavior."*

Logical consequences are related to the infraction. Fletcher did not stay on the home block when riding his bike so the bike is taken away for a day. Effective logical consequences require consideration, knowledge of your child and planning.

Parents know that the real world is a very misty gray area. Sometimes you just can't come up with a consequence that is either natural or logically related to the infraction. If Rufus will not get off his happy hiney and take out the overflowing garbage, then it's you who suffers the natural consequence – overflowing garbage. Rufus is quite content with his video game and may even be getting a little kick out of the idea that he is the inspiration for your hands on hips and squinty glaring eyes...as he looks up with an ever so innocent, "Whaaaat?"

An **imposed consequence** could be removing a privilege – bordering on a punishment by definition. The video game is turned off; the bike is taken away, whatever means something to Rufus. In order to stay out of the category of a punishment, the *consequence*:

- ♡ Should be based on a predetermined rule with agreed upon outcomes.
- ♡ Should not be arbitrary, unreasonable or punitive.
- ♡ Your child must understand he is making a choice by ignoring the rule or request.

Rufus should be reminded *once* that the garbage is full. If he doesn't respond, *matter-of-factly* the game goes away for however many hours/days/weeks you said it would. Yeah, "It's not fair!" "You're soooo mean!" "I'm gonna go live at Marcus' house!" Saying "Go!" might feel great in the moment, but choosing communication that kick starts his thinking brain such as, "What was our agreement about the garbage?" or, "What could you do differently next time so it doesn't happen again?" will better serve long term goals. Solutions like letting the garbage sit, "just till this part is over," or, "ten more minutes" are not an option (there is a pause button). Acceptable solutions are your decision. That is authoritative parenting.

When consequences are implemented with a calm, "No hard feelings, that's just the way it is" and, "Let's figure out what happened and how to make it better next time," approach, not only does the behavior improve, but the relationship can become stronger and more respectful in the long run. Afterward, check in with yourself (and your partner) to assess what your child learned from the encounter. Hopefully, it's what you intended, but as always, consider any unintentional lessons your actions may have taught and if there is anything you could change to expand the positive outcome next time.

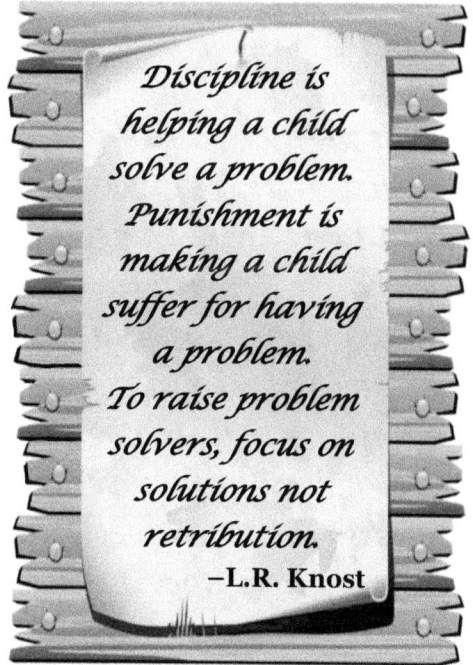

> *Discipline is helping a child solve a problem. Punishment is making a child suffer for having a problem. To raise problem solvers, focus on solutions not retribution.*
> —**L.R. Knost**

Choose your battles. Be absolutely sure when you make a request, describe an unacceptable situation, or remind about a rule, that you are ready, willing and able to follow through on your plan. *Do not* apologize for appropriate discipline. Express confidence that next time will be different, and that he can learn from this mistake. When there is a change or any attempt at change, notice the try and clearly and simply state your feelings, "It was hard, but you made a good choice."

Effective Consequences

Not only must you be committed to following through, your action must have sufficient meaning. When you're considering possible consequences, use your knowledge of what motivates your child to plan *effective* consequences. "Effective" means your response has enough meaning to motivate a change in behavior. If you keep trying the same thing and fail to get change, you are teaching your child that you are OK with being ignored and that he does not have to do as you ask. Again, *repetition makes your words and you, meaningless.* If you are taking away TV time because Percy has not mowed the lawn, and he's still not doing it, maybe removal of his video games will have more impact. Always expect positive behavior, but have ammunition (consequences) tucked in your saddle bags and don't be afraid to use them! If your action does not result in change, you have to be prepared to up the ante until it does.

> *"Whatever your horse is doing at this moment is what he is motivated to do. You must find what it takes to motivate change. If what you are doing does not result in change, you are training her to ignore – and have less and less respect for your authority."*

When you need to up the ante, in order to stay out of punishment territory, try including your child in crafting a solution. State the facts, "You haven't mowed the lawn." Then ask, "What do *you* suggest I do (take away, etc.) that will motivate you to do your part, because not doing it is not an option?" Having asked, you could get some charmingly ridiculous answers, but, your effort at collaboration could result in solutions you hadn't thought of. You might even get a little extra co-operation since you've made it clear you are not going to back off and you've valued their input by inviting collaboration. They may even exercise a little perspective taking because they have to put themselves in your place in order to come up with answers. Consequences that include children's own ideas either prior to or during an incident are more memorable to them.

On Time-out

Is traditional time-out a punishment or a consequence? Research tells us that an attachment-based approach that focuses on strengthening the parent/child relationship is more successful than behavioral approaches (such as time-out) in changing children's behavior. Success using traditional time-out is usually short lived and like any punishment, tends to damage the relationship.

If a time-out is used as a logical consequence such as, "I can see you need some time-out to calm yourself." Or, if a child needs to be removed from a situation where he cannot control his behavior, and you remove him with an explanation such as, "When you're ready to stop throwing sand, you can go back into the sand box," a time-out from the situation can be effective. If you feel you need a temporary technique to control out of bounds behavior and choose to use time-out in the traditional way, do not use it for children under three and not for more than four minutes.

On Spanking

"Over time, across cultures and ethnicities, the findings are consistent. Spanking is doing real, measurable damage to the brains of our children. It is associated with aggression, delinquency, mental health problems, and something called 'hostile attribution bias,' which essentially causes children to expect people to be mean to them.

"There's no study that I've ever done that's found a positive consequence of spanking. Most of us will stop what we're doing if somebody hits us, but that doesn't mean we've learned why somebody hit us, or what we should be doing instead, which is the real motive behind discipline."

Elizabeth Gershoff - associate professor at the University of Texas at Austin, who has been studying corporal punishment for 15 years, and is known as the leading researcher on spanking in the United States today.

Each time I spank, I'm teaching, "When you're angry, hit." I've never known of a child who was spanked into becoming a more loving human being.
-Hiam Ginott

> ### Ground Work 11 – Punishment or Consequence?
>
> Describe a particularly difficult incident when your child was defiant. Again, pick one that you think may be repeated.
>
> - Write an example of a *punishment* for the behavior and what thoughts might be going through your child's head if you were to use it.
>
> - Write two examples of *consequences*, the second a step up in intensity from the first, for the same behavior. Write what you would say and how and when you would implement them.
>
> - What might he/she be thinking afterwards? Consider what your child would learn from each interaction.

Because I Said So!

There are situations where co-operation is not feasible and a firm, "because I said so" is in order. Sometimes, "No" should simply mean "*No.*" Elizabeth Pantley in her informative and practical book, *Kid Cooperation*, describes three reasons you might need to just say, "No:"

1. **Your child is asking a question that she already knows the answer to** and is looking for a way to stall. Odelia has asked, "Why," 237 times, succeeding in buying herself five more minutes of Sponge Bob. Success!

2. **You've made a parental decision and the reason is just too complex for a child to understand.** Seven year old Bluebell wants to buy short shorts like the other girls are wearing. You have stated a well-considered, "No" and included the brief explanation that

short shorts are inappropriate for a seven year old. This inspires more intense argument and pleading, so mom's, "I see that you're angry, but I said no," needs to end the conversation.

3. **Giving the reason will just cause endless argument**. Wolfgang offers up the ever popular, "Whyyyy?" (Or, "Yeah, but...," "Can't we...?" "But, I don't want to," or "I HATE _____.") He doesn't really want to know why or to discuss personal preferences, he wants to wear you down and get you to change your mind. The more reasons you give, the harder he'll try and, "Because I said so!" again, needs to end it.

> *"You need to be assertive. Always offer the 'good deal," but, do something about the situation when it needs to be done. Be as gentle as possible but as firm as necessary."*

The more you respond or explain yourself in any of these situations, the more you are filling that bucket with negative attention and feeding the arguing beast! If the timing seems right, you could add an honest, "I'm just tired of answering that question." Then make *no further comment*.

On occasion, there may just not be time to go into an explanation, and you need to deliver a, "Because I said so" *and* add that you'll explain later, and then do so.

Children *should* know that there will be those times when they need to simply accept your answer. However, forcing a behavior change through pure authoritarian control only *seems* to work in the moment. When weighing the pros and cons of a "Because I said so" moment, consider your child's take away lesson. Could you lessen any negative messages with a short conversation later that helps her understand your decision making process? She may not agree, and you want to be clear this isn't an invitation to argue, but you will have respected her feelings and offered an opportunity for her to understand and respect yours. Never use "Because I said so," just because it's easier.

Ground Work 12 – Co-operation

- Describe an incident where your response to a request from your child was, "Because I said so!" Select a behavior that tends to be repeated.
- Write one or two clarifying (why, how, what if) questions you could have asked to learn more about the request. "Why do you ask?" "If I say yes, what will Mike's parents do?"
- Describe steps you might have taken to engage your child's thinking, logical brain in order to come to a mutually agreeable solution.
- Write two possible solutions.
- What would your child learn from each?

   Try out your solutions at the next opportunity and observe your child's response.

Are You Teaching the Fine Art of Manipulation?

Like Katie and Big Mamma in Chapter 1, it is chillingly easy to unknowingly teach the art of manipulation. First time mom, Morgan is aware that it is well past time for three year old Rosebud to give up the bottle. She rationalizes, "It only has

> *"Horses are great people trainers. All they have to do is rear up and get pushy, the person backs off and they get the comfort they crave."*

diluted juice in it and it keeps her quiet in the car and helps her calm down and get to sleep at night." When Morgan tries to explain to Rosebud that she is too grown-up for a bottle and attempts to leave it home or not give it to her at night, Rosebud escalates into a window rattling, tonsil showing fit. At first it was mild objection.

At two years old, Rosebud's M.O. was, "No, Mommy, I waaant it. Peeeeease!....Thank you, Mommy. I wove you." Ahhh, blessed quiet and, oh, the heartwarming sight of that adorable smile around the bottle below those twinkling brown eyes.

Morgan spent the next year seeking and following the advice of friends who assured her that a bottle for a three-year-old is not that bad, "She'll give it up when she's ready." With her dentist's warnings in mind, Morgan made several futile attempts to take the bottle away. She hardly noticed the escalating intensity of Rosebud's resistance with every attempt. *Rosebud successfully trained Morgan to back off* while learning that she could manipulate her mother with whining and resistance.

I used to tell the parents of young children I worked with to add ten years to their child's age and visualize how the current problem behavior looks and feels with ten more years of steady progression. Can you just picture thirteen year old Rosebud in her goth make-up, see-through top and short shorts when her mom says no to that tribal neck tattoo that she says all the other girls have convinced their parents to allow?

It's okay, in fact it's a good thing, if your child at times thinks (and loudly informs you and most of the other parents dropping off in front of the school) that you're just the meanest mommy or daddy *ever*! It's a sign you are being consistent, insistent and not being manipulated. Wear it proudly!

It is possible to misinterpret or take "seeking to understand," and "coming to a solution together," too far. Understanding feelings and co-operation does *not* equal allowing yourself to be manipulated. **Understanding the reason behind a negative behavior does not excuse it.**

In one of my riding lessons, Hannah was being especially fractious, and I just couldn't understand why. I'd ruled out lameness and other major discomforts. (This is critical to this concept. If your child is sick or truly traumatized, "suck-it-up," obviously does not apply.) Finally, I guessed Hannah might be hungry and cranky because I'd taken her away from her breakfast to do the lesson. My trainer, Anita said, **"That may be an explanation, but it's not an excuse for bad behavior."** Just gotta love those horse people.

"You need to have understanding and empathy, but excess here can get you into trouble. There may be an understandable explanation, but it's not an excuse to continue bad behavior."

We hear and empathize with Claudia, who does not like her teacher, hates math, and wants to punch Henrietta, but she still needs to put forth her best effort in class, get help in math and find a way to get along with Henrietta that doesn't involve spurting blood! Don't we adults have to do these things in our work environments? As a parent, you *should* try to understand and empathize with an explanation, but do not accept it as an excuse for bad behavior or poor decisions.

> *"When you lack confidence in yourself, your horse knows."*

I've heard many concerned parents ask if they will cause low self-esteem, insecurity, depression, anger, limited creativity or lack of self-expression, etc., in their children if they are firm in setting and enforcing rules or have high expectations. *When rules and expectations are age appropriate and clearly understood in advance by all parties, they should be consistently upheld.* Children are experts at knowing what buttons to push in order to get the reaction and the decision they want. Parents have to become experts at discerning when they are being "worked" and when there is that very real, but rare, physical or emotional issue that needs extra support. Remember, testing those rules and expectations is normal; it's not something you have control over. You do have control over your own response.

Kids with little or no tolerance for delayed gratification or disappointment can evolve when parents allow themselves to be manipulated by guilt or even a child who is just testing. The outcome can be manipulative personality traits such as "guilt tripping" others, using subversive and/or obvious threats, blaming others for one's own bad behavior, bullying and its flip side, playing the victim, and of course, my all-time favorite, an overdeveloped sense of entitlement. "I *deserve* this, just because I *am*...and I *want* it!"

> **Children are not equipped and should not be permitted to wield manipulative power in their relationships with caregivers.**

Some children who have succeeded in growing their power and control through manipulation, especially teens, learn to further manipulate by intentionally withdrawing from their parents. *Do not fall into the trap of trying to appease in order to avoid "losing" your child!* In my experience children that exhibit the obnoxious behaviors that result from being allowed to manipulate do not need *more* privileges, analysis of fears and insecurities or help with poor self-esteem. They need an assertive, involved parent that will consistently enforce limits and use true discipline. Children are not equipped and should not be permitted to wield manipulative power in their relationships with caregivers. The unintentional lessons can build lifelong patterns that lead to negative and failed relationships.

The Co-operation Process

Co-operation is the two (or more) of you reviewing the facts of a conflict or incident and coming to a mutually agreeable solution together. Standing by, wine glass in hand, watching those convenient natural consequences happen is sadly *not* enough for true learning to take place. Even enforcing consequences is not enough. All involved parties should review the sequence of events of an incident, including choices made and consequences implemented. Discuss feelings and possible solutions. These are the five cooperative steps of co-operation that will turn a mistake into a lasting learning experience:

1. Describe the issue simply and without accusation or judgement. If your child is old enough, have her participate in laying out the basics of what happened.

2. Review the thought processes that went into her choices by asking open-ended, clarifying questions that don't place blame or ridicule. *Listen.* Ask questions that help her explore the results of her choices.

3. Ask what *she* thinks should be done to achieve more positive results if a similar situation arises again. Offer up some possible solutions. They don't all have to be good ones, just brainstorm together.

4. For each possible solution, ask, "What would happen if we/you _____?" How do you see that working out?

5. Work together to choose the best option, then put the responsibility for follow-through on your child. Let her know you will be there to support her by honoring your portion of the agreement and that you fully expect her to honor hers.

A confident and consistent parent who can promote cooperation without manipulation will support positive decision making and taking personal responsibility for one's own actions. You also demonstrate how interacting with the intent to find a win-win solution builds good relationships.

> *The level of cooperation parents get from their children is usually equal to the level of connection children feel with their parents.*
> **Racheous.com**

On Tantrums

The advice parents often hear is to ignore tantrums, which may or may not work, depending on your goal in responding. The first order of business is to determine a cause if possible. Identify any logical reasons – is he tired, hungry, getting sick, frustrated, over stimulated? Then, distinguish between the two basic types of tantrum in order to respond appropriately.

Type 1, the, **"I want my way and I'm gonna flip out till I get it"** tantrum. She can stop if she wants to but she is using a tantrum to manipulate. This must receive the, "Never negotiate with a terrorist" response! Let her know you understand her feelings and inform her of her choices and their consequences, *one time!* Then wait. What you ignore is any arguing, whining, screaming, flailing or attempts to bargain. If possible don't even look at her. When her thinking brain makes an appearance, and she is relatively calm and able to reason, you can discuss better ways to ask for what she wants and to get her needs met. She will learn that her bad choice in behavior does not work and she can survive delayed gratification. She will stop using tantrums to get her way because she's received minimal attention and it simply didn't work.

Type 2, an **"emotional melt-down tantrum"** is when any of the underlying physical causes mentioned above are present or the pressures of just being a two year old become too much and the emotional portions of the brain completely take over (screaming, kicking, hitting, throwing himself down), rendering him *incapable* of any higher order thinking skills. If there is danger of injury or destruction, you may need to physically hold and/or remove him from the scene. When it's safe, a nurturing, calming connection is the first order of business. Help calm him by identifying and naming his emotions. Once the logical, reasoning brain is engaged and receptive, discuss his feelings and behavior, and then explore acceptable ways to express those feelings. He will learn that he *can* calm himself, he *can* express anger or fear or panic or just plain not feeling good in ways that will get positive results.

"Really concentrate on the details of your relationship with your horse. Are you babying him too much and giving him treats? Are you sometimes compromising, 'Oh well, I guess you don't really have to do that right now.' Does he move out of your space or does he bump into you and rub his head on you? These are all symptoms that the horse has not truly accepted your authority."

CHAPTER 7

PRINCIPLE 5, CONSISTENCY

"Every second, you are either schooling or unschooling your horse. There is no in-between."

Consistent, Clear and Fair

Mark Rashid said, *"With horses and with humans, the way to develop trust is with consistency."* Within reason, rules and expectations should be enforced across all situations and circumstances. Whether you are at home, the grocery, the movies, the park, or grandmas, whether it is mom, dad, a teacher, or the babysitter, whether you or your child are sick, tired, frustrated, in a hurry, celebrating, sad or angry, the basic rules of interaction must always be upheld. This principle is the foundation of authoritative parenting.

Its annoyingly easy to let an opportunity to teach a positive lesson slip by or to unintentionally teach a negative one. Let's say the rule is for Lola to put her toys away before moving on to a new activity. Lola is so quietly coloring, that Mom just goes ahead and tosses the building blocks in their tub because it's easier and quicker than facing the inevitable battle over getting Lola to pick them up. Every time Mom makes what seems to be a minor exception like this, a pattern is reinforced in Lola's brain supporting the idea that not only does she not really need to follow *this* rule, but that rules in general are flexible and only apply when convenient. How will that lesson sit with mom when applied to situations like curfew times, homework, dating, driving, drinking, drugs, or sex? Consistency is the key. Take advantage of following through on the little things and you'll minimize confrontations over the big ones.

> **Consistency is key. Follow through on the little things and you'll minimize confrontations over the big ones.**

Expectations must be clear and fair as well as consistent to be effective. If the answer to a test is *unclear*, your child will need to test again, maybe in a different way, and usually with increased intensity.

The first time Elmer presents mom with the flowers he picked from Mrs. Chang's yard without permission, she gives him a hug and says, "Oh, no, Elmer, you shouldn't pick Mrs. Chang's flowers." Then mom walks away with a big smile as she sniffs the flowers and puts them in her favorite vase. Little Elmer has no clue if he should be picking the flowers or not. He'll have to try again, and he may need to pick a few more for clarity. Like horses, kids do not handle incongruence well. Words and actions must match.

If a parent's answers are consistent and clear but unfair, the resulting anger, hurt and frustration can turn into resentment and rebellious behavior. If this is a pattern over time, ugly characteristics and a possible lifetime of conflict, personality disorders and miserable relationships can develop.

Three year-old Regina also finds Mrs. Chang's garden irresistible, picks some flowers and has a good old time playing in the dirt while she's at it. When her embarrassed father discovers her, he reacts with the admirable intent of "teaching her a lesson," but dragged her into the house while delivering a swat on the behind and angrily admonishing her for getting dirty *and* trashing Mrs. Chang's garden. He tells her to stay in her room and think about what she's done.

I'd bet a little peek inside Regina's mind would reveal anger, sadness and resentment, with very little of dad's hoped for remorse. His reaction very clearly showed his displeasure with her actions, but held no consideration of Regina's motives, developmental level or the unintentional lessons he has now taught. He made no attempt to acknowledge feelings or connect. What did his actions teach Regina about how to handle anger, about how to control another person's behavior, about how *she* should expect to be treated? She may not go back into that garden, but what effects will this experience and the many similar ones before and after it have on her relationship with her dad?

> *"Build on trust; true leadership is built on calm firmness and consistency, not force or dominance."*

What lessons might Regina have learned if there was a rule with a known consequence about Mrs. Chang's garden or if her dad had approached the incident as a teachable moment using the Connect, Communicate and Co-operate process? Some unintentional lessons have longer lasting cumulative effects than others.

You are Always Teaching!

Kids learn from *everything* you say and do, your actions or inaction, your attitude and words, intentional or not, positive or negative. And they seem to learn the emotionally charged unintentional lesson much quicker than the intentional. If you rant on, you teach them to tune out. If you yell and lose your temper or hit, they learn to yell and lose their temper and hit. If you take a deep breath and *respond* with teaching in mind, they learn to control their own impulses. If you listen, they learn to listen. If you are thoughtful, confident, fair, and, consistent, chances are your child will grow into a responsible adult who exhibits the characteristics you listed in Ground Work 1.

Model integrity and kindness. If you want your children to be happy, healthy, contributing members of society, research shows they must be taught to be kind to others. Discuss your charitable acts when you do them, not for a pat on the back, but to let your children in on your thought process. Ask them questions about how others might feel, especially those on the fringes or the outcasts at school. If another child is being disruptive in class, ask why he thinks he may be doing that. A group of boys playing ball intentionally hit little Billy with the ball that knocks off his glasses. Encourage discussion about how he might feel and how they might safely intervene to make Billy's day a bit better. Be pro-active and bring up hypothetical situations.

Plan to do a random act of kindness once a week or a month, together, then discuss how great it feels to be kind, and how the recipient may have felt. Promote kind attitudes and actions in your children by *acknowledging their actions and the value it represents.* "I bet Colleen was really grateful you shared your sandwich with her on the field trip. That was a very caring thing to do."

You are always teaching or un-teaching virtues such as honesty, humility, empathy, honor, gratitude and compassion. Think of what lessons your child learns if he overhears you tell your boss you are not coming in to work because you are sick when you're not. If you are an honest, respectful person, your children will respect you. True respect is earned, never forced.

The media has a huge impact on children, especially pre-teens and teens. It's OK to be a helicopter parent when it comes to the messages your child is receiving from media! Monitor what they watch. Just because, "all my friends are watching it," doesn't mean your child should. There's no way around it, exposure to media influences your children's character and it's up to you what they watch and what games they play. You aren't the only one who is always teaching.

> **You aren't the only one who is always teaching.**

Ask open-ended and clarifying questions about what your kids have watched or heard in media, music, school, church or from friends. Observe and listen for the impact it's having on their character. A teacher friend of mine said she could always tell when "Bad Girls Club" had aired, because the girls in class who had seen it were skillfully imitating the dress, language and attitudes they had seen the night before. Make informed decisions and *stick with them.*

Ground Work 13 - Do Some Ground Work *Together*

As soon as your child is old enough to communicate, role-play with him and rehearse what you would say and what he would say in pretend situations. Use dolls, stuffed animals, action figures or puppets, even sticks can be characters. Act out familiar or potentially volatile scenarios, some fun and some difficult. "Look, this mommy needs to go to the store, but little Wilhelmina doesn't want to go. What can they do?" "Herbert is really angry because his dad said he can't buy the toy truck today, and he's screaming! What should his daddy say?" Talk about how the characters feel. Discuss what learning is taking place in the situation. Connect the scenario to her life. "Have you ever felt frustrated like Herbert? What do you think you should do when you feel that way?"

Breathe, Think, Then Answer

Say yes as often as you can and save no for when you really need it and "No" will have more meaning. Being a strong leader often means choosing the more difficult path. If saying "Yes" is easy, "No" is probably what's needed. If saying "No" is easy, "Yes" may be best. Wimp out, and testing behaviors *will* escalate and your hard earned leadership will be undermined.

On Thursday, Alfreda asks, "Dad, can I spend the night with Violet tonight?" This is the pivotal moment when Dad should take a breath, think, ask some clarifying questions and consider carefully. Whether he decides to say yes or no, he must be committed to sticking with it! If he changes his mind or gives in to objections or pleas, he will have just taught Alfreda to argue! Alfreda's note to self would be: "I can get Dad to bend the rules and change his mind if I am persistent in arguing and throw in a little pleading and whining." And Dad shouldn't be surprised when she tries again at the very next opportunity since he has taught her so well.

> When you are doing the job right, there will be many times when your children dislike you. Yay! It means you are striving to be a responsible parent, not just a popular parent! The difference in this type of reactive anger and the deep resentment that comes with consistent arbitrary punishment is in the intensity of the emotion fueled by the feeling of unfairness and helplessness. Implementing agreed upon rules and their consequences may not endear you in the moment, but it's not mean or thoughtless. If connection and caring is your pattern, you have built a trusting relationship that can withstand the enforcement of consequences.

Dad knows his daughter and if he says "No" to her, she will want to know "Whhhyyyyy noooot?" She will argue, "Maggie is going. You never let me go! You treat me like a baby." He knows how that comment twists his gut so he rehearses some responses.

Even though it's a week night and the rule is no overnights on week nights, it would be so much easier to say yes and take blissful joy in her bouncy, happy face instead of a snarling, "You are soooo mean!" But, every single time Dad takes the easy way by giving in, agreeing or permitting, even in what may seem like the most insignificant incidence, he is reinforcing the perception that he is a weak leader and a push-over.

"It's the 997 little things that make the big difference. Lipping leads to nipping which leads to biting."

Alfreda's dad, however, is no wimp. He listened and let Alfreda know he heard, then carefully considered. He knows he has to say "No," and stick to it. He delivers his chosen rehearsed response aloud to Alfreda. And...this is why he loves his new wireless, sound deadening ear buds.

Like Alfreda's dad, you can give yourself an injection of strength by fully utilizing Principle 1, *Consider*. Predict your child's typical reactions in different situations and practice delivering the unpopular answer. Visualize what his reaction would be, then rehearse some effective responses, including silence. Proper preparation precedes peak performance.

Now, I hesitate to even include this next comment because it can easily be misinterpreted as license to give in. It *is* admitedly a fine line. **Consistency does not mean rigidity**. If you decide to make a rare, *well-considered* concession to a reasonably presented (without whining) request for an exception to a rule or decision, clearly and simply explain why and go with it. Your kids need to know you're not arbitrary, that you don't have an overdeveloped need to be right, that you're paying attention to their feelings and willing to reason. Consider the details, circumstances and repercussions carefully *before* you answer.

> *Our children are counting on us to provide two things: consistency and structure. Children need parents who say what they mean, mean what they say, and do what they say they are going to do.*
> -Barbara Coloroso

Counting With Horse Sense

Have you ever heard parents use counting to three as a threat to get their child to behave? Doesn't work; don't do it. Those children are learning to listen and respond to the count, and *not* their parent's request. Here's what counting to three *should* look like:

1. **State the facts**, "Bernice, it's time to come in." If no success;

2. **Ask again with a statement of the consequences,** emphasizing she *is* making a choice, "Time to come inside now, Bernice or I will come get you, *your choice.*"

3. If you still don't get the response you want, **follow through with the consequence.** Go out, take Bernice by the hand and gently but firmly help her inside. Either say nothing or simply state, *one time,* "You chose to stay out when I asked you to come in, so now I'll help you come in."

"There is a theory in cueing horses called "Ask - Tell - Command." It means that the first time you ask a horse to do something, you ask gently and politely. The second time you make the point with greater authority. The third time, you let the horse know you really mean business with a corrective action. If you are asking beyond 3 times, you are training your horse to ignore your directives."

Ignore *all* pleading, arguing and crying. Don't let her see the steam coming out of your ears! You're the picture of "cool, calm and collected."

If this is a repeated behavior and your child clearly understands the rule and the consequences of ignoring it from the beginning, she is manipulating. **Skip step two and go right to step three**. The goal is for Bernice to respond to the first, "as gentle as possible" request. It *will* happen when consequences are consistently enforced.

What unintentional lessons does the other version of counting to three teach?

The Continuum

Consistent interactions with children create patterns in their brains that become a continuum they are compelled to repeat. In riding, the most desirable behavior pattern is called "softness." A "soft" horse responds instantly to the slightest cue or suggestion from the rider. The rider can almost *think* "trot" and the horse trots. This is accomplished by first establishing leadership with the horse. Then, requests are always asked as politely and softly as possible. If needed, our rider will step up the intensity of the request, then, if necessary, use a light corrective action. The horse quickly learns to respond to the first, gentle request and this becomes his pattern. He learns softness as his continuum, his "way of going," and he seeks the comfort of that continuum as he learns more and more difficult maneuvers.

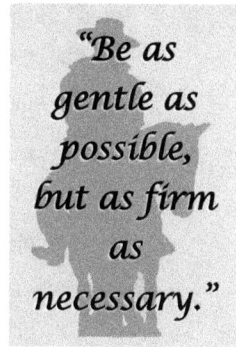

"Be as gentle as possible, but as firm as necessary."

In contrast, a horse treated roughly learns to respond only to force and a heavy hand and will ignore a soft request. He will never *willingly* achieve more advanced levels.

With children, the patterns you create affect all areas of their lives. If the continuum you've created is one of understanding and gentleness balanced with consistency, they will be motivated to stay on that familiar path by seeking out and demonstrating strength, understanding and gentleness in their relationships. If their continuum is force, anger, or any degree of violence (including verbal), *even though unpleasant*, they will continue to be drawn to and give the same. Think of those who repeat the pattern of abusive relationships even though they were subjected to the pain of abuse as children. There is an innate desire to live within a familiar continuum and to find comfort in those patterns, be they positive or negative.

There are notable exceptions to this premise. Some people succeed with positive change by recognizing the need to change and acting on a commitment to doing whatever it takes to learn a new "way of going." (See Buck Brannaman, page 175.)

A variety of continuums are played out in school settings. Children from different styles of family continuums find themselves in an environment where only soft or respectful communication is acceptable. Is it the fault of the child who has lived a pattern of heavy handedness that he's clueless about softness? Is his parent to blame if that was also his or her continuum? Patterns can be traced back for generations. The continuum only shifts when a parent makes a conscious decision to break the chain and does the ground work needed to create lasting change. And when it does, it also shifts for future generations.

Let's Review the Pattern - For Consistency

When a teachable moment rears its head, you have:

- ♡ **Considered** - Done your pre-moment ground work by observing and predicting your child's typical reactions and what calms him. You are grounded in your authority as a parent and know your own reactions. You have a general plan for what you want your child to learn and how best to teach it. You have thought through possible consequences should they be needed.

- ♡ **Connected** – Built a strong loving relationship, will listen and acknowledge feelings. You will connect to your child's thinking brain through his emotional brain to help him move toward a reasoning, thinking frame of mind.

- ♡ **Communicated** – Asked clarifying questions and listened some more. If applicable, you implemented consequences, all while keeping your cool.

♡ **Co-operated** – You will problem solve and come to a solution together with your child, with *you* making the final decision on appropriateness.

♡ **Consistency** – You will be consistent in your enforcement of your clear and fair expectations.

Let's revisit the situation with little Zeke in the Forward, who ran off in Marshalls to play Hide-n-Seek in the jeans racks. First, judging by mom's tone, this is not the first time he's done this. Mom could have first considered Zeke's age and temperament and how long he could reasonably be expected to stay with her while she shopped. (A two year old should not be expected to stand quietly for more than two minutes in a store! A four to five year old, maybe for a half hour). *She should have thought through what might happen and considered some preventative measures and appropriate consequences ahead of time.*

If Zeke was young and small enough, Mom might have had him sit in the cart with a toy while shopping if he was not able to keep himself near her. Or he might have needed to hold mom's hand. They might both have gone to go sit in the car with no toys, music or video games until he was ready to stay near her, whatever would be the most effective approach for Zeke.

She *could have had a discussion with Zeke before they left home, clearly laying out what her expectations were for his behavior, including a description of the consequences should he choose not to comply.* If Zeke expressed an honest, "I HATE going

to Marshalls!" *mom might have agreed to bring along a favorite toy and/or offer a time limit and/or a trip to the park afterwards to show she is listening and reasonable.* If Zeke is over three years old, mom should not repeat the expectations and consequences. Once the expectation is stated, his behavior is his responsibility.

Mom should expect him to comply, but be ready to support him when necessary. For example, when Zeke chose to make his first escape, mom should have caught him before he got far. *She should have brought him back and reminded him **once** of the possible consequences.* When he ran off again, it was time to *implement the consequence with a brief reminder of the agreement,* ignoring all protests. When he was calm, maybe on the way home (no park, if that was the pre-trip agreement), there should have been *a review of what happened and choices made and then a cooperative agreement on behavioral expectations for the next trip.*

The processes of connecting, communicating and co-operating should not be interpreted as weakness or per-missiveness. They are meant to help you maintain a balance between strong leadership and compassionate connection. Cooperative agreements must fall within your reasonable expectations of appropriate behavior. You'll teach taking responsibility for one's own actions and positive, productive balance in relationships.

Ground Work 14 – "Zeke!"

Consider the example of little Zeke in the Forward.

- Write down every unintentional lesson Zeke might have learned from the original description of the way mom dealt with him that day in the store.

- Consider the "Mom could have" statements in italics on the previous pages and write what Zeke might have learned from each step.

- With repeated similar interactions throughout childhood, consider how Zeke might behave as a teenager in each example of parenting.

- Make some guesses as to what characteristics you might use to describe him as an adult in each instance.

- How do you think Zeke will grow to parent his children in each instance?

Make a Plan

The best tool you have for maintaining emotional control is planning ahead. When a situation erupts and you have no plan in mind, your thinking brain is not prepared, so your primitive survival brain and right brain team up to react however they deem best. When you run out of knowledge to guide you, emotions like fear, frustration, anger, or anxiety rule reactions.

At this point in this book, you should:

♡ Have a generalized understanding of how children's brains work,

💟 Know your own and your child's temperament and how they interact together,

💟 Have explored your expectations and rules,

💟 Know when and what types of misbehavior are likely to occur.

We have come full circle, back to "Consider." It's time to make a parenting plan. Think of a situation where your child's typical reaction is to bring on the ugly. Consider what precise behavior you want to change and what you want him to learn, then plan what you will say and do in order to teach it using the pattern *"Connect, Communicate and Co-operate."* Try to predict every possible "what if." What techniques will you use to connect? What clarifying questions will you ask? Think of effective natural or logical consequences that you are ready, willing and able to implement should they become necessary. What solutions might you consider as you discuss the event afterwards? Might there be unintentional negative lessons?

For example, let's say you've taken into careful consideration your three-year-old daughter Henrietta's budding independence and know she will insist on wearing the most outlandish outfit possible for preschool tomorrow. Your goal is for her to learn to make appropriate clothing choices for school and to accept that when you give a directive or offer a limited choice, you will not be deterred. Your plan is to present her with options that are within your acceptable parameters (an excellent strategy for two to five year olds entrenched in the process of establishing their autonomy), so you've selected two outfits for her to choose from. Knowing Henrietta, you predict she will communicate their unacceptability with crossed arms, brow lines touching the bridge of her nose and a loud, "I *HATE* those stupid clothes," and she'll go to the closet and pull out the rainbow tutu, those green and orange striped tights and purple dress-up heels that she dearly loves. You also predict this would normally fire up your fury reaction, so you have planned and rehearsed some calming techniques.

> *"Observe, remember, and compare. Do something when it needs to be done, remember what you did, compare it to what you were doing before, and adjust. Interact with temperament and uniqueness in mind."*

You've learned that showing her that you heard her by listening to and restating her objections will help her focus and connect. You've rehearsed acknowledging her feelings with comments like, "You don't like the outfits I picked out and want to wear your tights and heels." You know that all you'll need is a "Yes," to confirm you are connected to her thinking brain, and can then attempt logical communication.

You'll explain that the heels are not safe to wear at school and against school rules and remind her she must choose between the outfits you have picked out. Predicting that this may still be unacceptable to her, you've considered some consequences. You could say, "If you can't make a decision, I'll choose" or, "We leave in five minutes. If you don't decide by then, you'll go to school in your pajamas." (Now, you've really got to know your kid. Going to school in pajamas might be a blast for one, horrendous to another!)

The important thing is to be in control of your emotions and the situation. You'll put on your firm and matter-of-fact mask and will be absolutely committed to following through on whatever consequences you've decided ahead of time are fair and effective. Again, never start what you're not willing to finish.

You'll explain, *one time only,* your reasons for implementing the consequence. You will calmly ignore all whining, crying, arguing, pleading, etc. You know that if you get sucked into an argument or react with frustration or anger, you'll be giving attention to negative behaviors and teaching her that she can manipulate you and gain control by using them. Experiencing consequences in a matter-of-fact way will teach her the value of making decisions within your acceptable options and that you are in charge. Henrietta *will* learn that you cannot be manipulated or deterred from your rules or decisions. *You* rock!

Without a thought-out plan, the same scenario would likely include increased volume, a reddening face and declarations like, "No, you *cannot* wear that! I told you to wear this!" This might be answered with a loud, "No, I don't want to!" including crying, flailing, glaring and tears. We'd have reptile brain yelling at reptile brain, right brain to right brain, I win, you lose, and collateral damage to the relationship. This child may also eventually learn that she has to wear what her parent says, but there'd be no *positive* lessons about making choices or how to communicate or what kind of leader her mom is. Can you see other possible unintentional negative lessons in the "no plan" scenario?

You know spirited Henrietta will test Mom's resolve again and depending on her temperament, again and again. But each time the result will be more positive and that positive pattern will grow – assuming mom sticks to her guns and does not give in!

Sometimes, the best plan is to do nothing in order to take advantage of an opportunity for your child to learn problem solving skills. When you intentionally and consistently wait a beat to offer time for processing, your child will learn to take advantage of that moment of silence to think things through for himself. If you always jump in with help, offering a solution to the problem, why should he put energy into trying to find one?

If two children are fighting over a toy, instead of being super-mom or dad and jumping in to save the day with your super-solution, a better lesson may be learned if you hang back a bit and see if they can solve it on their own (up to the point of an emergency room visit). If you absolutely have to step in, acknowledge the feelings on both sides, without taking sides, and ask prompting questions to guide the combatants toward mutual agreement. Pronounce a parental solution only as a last resort. Both children will experience the opportunity to learn to solve problems themselves, which is the ultimate goal, yes?

"Sometimes people are so afraid of making mistakes, that the biggest mistake they make is doing nothing. You can't fix things by just showing them love."

I'm not talking here about doing nothing out of fear of doing the wrong thing or simply not having a plan. Sidney's dad discovered a container with a small amount of pot when vacuuming sixteen year old Sidney's room. Dad didn't know if he should confront Sidney about it and, if so, what would be the right thing to say, to do? Hoping it was just a harmless passing phase, he did nothing. Two weeks later Sidney was arrested for having "his friend's" three ounces of pot, a pipe, some pills and a large amount of cash in his backpack at the baseball game.

Buck Brannaman on children; "Give the child someplace to go, a way out, a choice. Give him something to do so that he can succeed. If you wait for him to do the wrong thing because you weren't paying attention to your responsibilities, and then become angry, he won't learn from the experience. He'll learn to fear you, learn to be sneaky and covert about what he does and he may never learn to do the right thing. Instead, he's likely to learn nothing but how to fail."

Sidney's dad should have considered Sidney's past behavior patterns and how best to approach the subject, then discussed with him what he'd found. Dad should have recognized a teaching opportunity and had a courageous life discussion about drugs, exploring what was going on in Sidney's world with as much calm as possible. Dad could have reiterated family expectations and the consequences of drug use, both within the family and society. If that conversation had taken place and Sidney still made the same bad choice, then the arrest would have been the natural consequence of Sidney's choices.

> **There is much to be gained by addressing difficult situations when they are a manageable size and way too much to lose by ignoring them and hoping for the best.**

There is much to be gained by consistently addressing difficult situations immediately, when they are more likely to be a manageable size and way too much to lose by ignoring them and hoping for the best. Fifteen years of my forty year career was spent supporting pregnant and parenting teens, so I've seen up close and very personal what happens when parents put the blinders on when it comes to uncomfortable potential danger signs. Parents must always be ready to teach and support when needed, which is rarely when it's convenient or expected. Dive in, even when the waters are unknown, uncomfortable or scary. Address an issue early *even if* you don't have a plan or find the topic terrifying. As soon as possible, address situations that you realize you have let get out of hand. Use the pattern Connect, Communicate, Co-operate and step up, be a consistent leader. Be the parent.

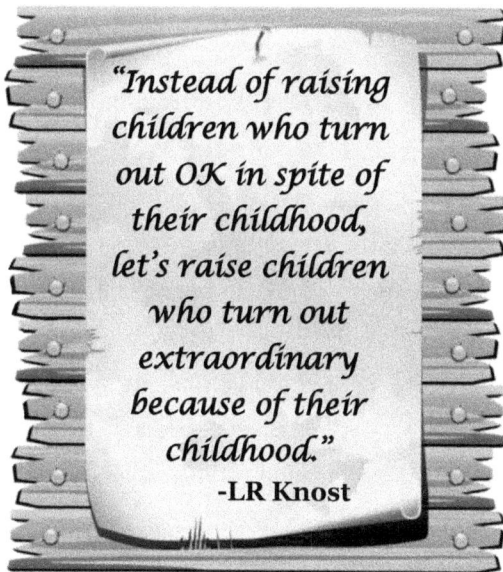

> *"Instead of raising children who turn out OK in spite of their childhood, let's raise children who turn out extraordinary because of their childhood."*
> -LR Knost

Ground Work 15 – Make the Five Mighty C's Yours

- Again, describe an incident where your child has misbehaved.
- Now write down "what happened before what happened, happened." What was the cause or precursor of the behavior?
- Honestly write how you *reacted* in as much detail as possible. What did you do and say that was successful in teaching what you intended? What about your actions helped to build your relationship? What did you do and say that supported your goals for your child?
- **Consider** your child's temperament, communication style and preferences, and write down what you want him/her to learn from the situation.
- Write a plan for how you could *respond* in the future:

 ♡ What words will you use to **connect**? What will you say and do?

 ♡ What questions will you ask to support **communication**? How will you show you have listened?

 ♡ What **consequences** will you implement if necessary? When and in what context will you discuss them beforehand?

 ♡ What collaborative steps could you take to promote **co-operation** in the future? What are some phrases you could use that will facilitate this process? What are some possible solutions?

- Review each step and list as many things as you can think of that your child will learn as your plan is implemented. Are there any possible negative lessons? If so, revise your plan.
- What concrete steps can you take to help yourself be **consistent**?

CHAPTER 8

LASSO CHANGE

Why Choose Change

I hear some folks saying, "My parents didn't do any of this stuff and I came out just fine, thank you very much!" Well, that *is* wonderful. *Take the Reins!* is not about being "good enough," it's about learning from current research as well as from the horse whisperers to optimize those teachable moments so your children are as mentally and emotionally prepared as possible for an ever changing and challenging new world. It's about being the best parent you can be.

It's important to examine whether or not you are offering opportunities for and intentionally teaching good decision making. Are you building the resiliency needed to cope with and embrace change in a quickly changing global and technologically entrenched world? In what ways is life for your child in today's society different than it was for you? What kinds of choices are they faced with that children from previous generations weren't?

Peter West (West 2004) states that "The web of confident, authoritative individuals that supported a parent in their efforts to guide children in times past is missing. Church, school, law enforcement, and others in the community could be counted on to reinforce family values. *Children buck weak authority to assert their need for stability in a world of wobbly values.*"

I believe it's not the institutions themselves that have changed as much as our attitudes toward them. Our litigious society has weakened many anchors of the community. There have been abuses, and corrections were and continue to be needed, but the pendulum has swung so far in the opposite direction that a society with diminishing common basic core values is evolving. If a person or family is not grounded in either traditional cultural values or values they have taken the time to thoughtfully select and define for themselves, they are like a ball in a pin-ball machine, bouncing wildly between media created value and random opinions. Could the need for belonging and for grounding in strong core beliefs be a contributing factor to why so many teens and young adults latch on to any bright, shiny answer they hit up against, even when the answer is radical, self-destructive or seems bizarre to their peers and family?

Many choices faced by families in our modern society were not even possibilities in previous generations. The media shoves products and choices in the faces of children who then can't possibly live without things that they otherwise wouldn't have known existed. In the "olden days," when I was a kid, when a child had a special desire, often the funds just weren't there to create a decision for their parents. Kids were forced to find another way. They used creative problem solving; they may even have worked for it, and learned some great life lessons by doing so! Not so much for today's kids. For many of them, well intentioned parents make their children's lives too easy for the right kinds of learning to take place. (See Afluenza, page 167) It is critical to increase your awareness that a behavior or request in front of you *is* a teachable moment that can be used to build resiliency and strength in your child. Fresh eyes and ears are needed just to approach every disciplinary decision not as a minor occurrence, to be handled dismissively, but a *choice* that adds another thread to the tapestry of your child's character.

It takes amazing self-awareness to check your emotions and weigh the long term pros and cons once a choice is recognized. The commitment to raising that child you described in Chapter 3 must be rock solid in order to make the decision to say to yourself, "I am not going to say yes, or give this to you, even though I can afford it, because I'm building your character!" When your answer to a request from your child supports this unpopular stand, the difficulty in sticking to it will no doubt be magnified under an unrelenting onslaught of creative arguments! It gets tougher as children grow older and even more aware that it may not be a matter your ability to afford whatever it is, but that you are *choosing* to say "No" for their own good. Your long term idea and your child's here and now idea of "his own good" are likely worlds apart.

> **Fresh eyes and ears are needed just to approach every disciplinary decision not as a minor occurrence, to be handled dismissively, but a *choice* that adds another thread to the tapestry of your child's character.**

The benefits to your child's developing character are enormous when you first recognize and then use every opportunity to let them safely experience failure and frustration when they are young and you are around to support their learning process. If breakfast is no longer being served at Burger King, don't accommodate by driving to McDonald's! Light bulb moment! This as an opportunity for little Abner to experience constructive disappointment. He'll have to make a different choice off of Burger King's menu and by doing so will learn to cope with disappointment, build emotional resilience, problem solving skills, the ability to delay gratification and to collaborate. And, he'll experience the character enhancing idea that he is not entitled to something just because he wants it. You couldn't manufacture such a valuable opportunity or buy an electronic toy to teach all of that for any price! And the situation was handed to you for free. All you have to do is recognize it as the amazing opportunity to teach that it is.

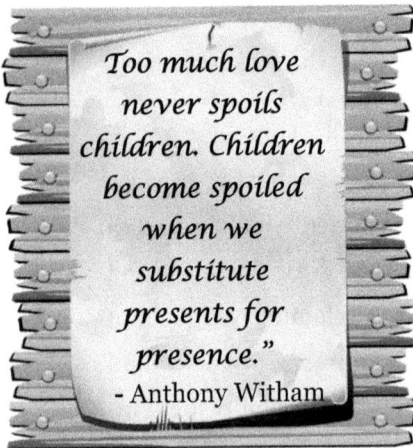

> *Too much love never spoils children. Children become spoiled when we substitute presents for presence."*
> — Anthony Witham

In the late 1960s, Walter Mischel of Stanford University conducted a now classic experiment about a child's ability to delay gratification. When children were offered the choice of taking either one marshmallow now, or two later, most kids chose the "two later" option. However, not all of them could stick to their decision when the experimenter left the room. Long term follow up has shown that the longer the children were able to wait at age four, the better their SAT scores and the better the ratings of their ability to control themselves and to pursue their academic and life goals successfully. The children who were least able to delay gratification were more likely to become bullies and have drug problems in adulthood. This is powerful stuff!

Georgina was struggling in her position as forward on her soccer team and told her dad that she desperately wanted to be the goalie. Instead of going with his first instinct which was to be super-dad and go talk with the coach and attempt to fix the problem for Georgina; her dad exchanged his cape for a thinking cap. Recognizing the choice, the opportunity to teach, he first helped Georgina to explore what it was she really wanted to do, and acknowledged her efforts to learn, to gain skills and to support her team. They created a plan together that included strategies for improving her skills. Because of her dad's choices, Georgina *didn't* learn that she is entitled to what she wants, or that others will fix her life when things get difficult. She *did* learn that her dad will understand her feelings and the situation and will support her in her efforts to improve. She learned that hard work and effort are how one gains desired skills.

Affluenza and Drones

One extreme result of failing to take advantage of learning opportunities has fondly been dubbed "Affluenza." It is a psychological adaptation previously affecting primarily the wealthy, but can be found today throughout the economic spectrum. The disease can be diagnosed in any family where the children have learned that they are entitled to everything they want and can be subtly insidious in the way it impacts parenting. It starts with love.

Because we love our children we understandably want only the absolutely most bountiful and happy life for them. Everyone wants their children to have nice things, clothes, cars, fun toys, vacations, horses, etc., and in today's modern society many parents can afford to just give it to them. The gift, however, is a Trojan horse. It is filled with a sense of entitlement, lack of motivation, laziness, a consistent need for immediate gratification, to be constantly entertained, and self-centeredness.

> *Don't handicap your children by making their lives easy."*
> -Robert A. Heinlein

Are you the parent who recognizes a request as an opportunity to teach and stops to ask yourself if it is in your child's best interest *in* the long run? Do you question the potential unintentional lessons hidden inside? If so, you will be the parent who supports the positive character goals you set for your child in Chapter 3.

If Orville's family (Forward) had worked out a plan with Orville for him to *earn* the money for a car instead of simply buying the new car *for* him, might Orville have valued the car more and been a bit more careful in his driving? What character building and useful life skills could Orville have gained if his parents exploited the teachable moment? What could he have learned if he was held accountable for his bad choices and had to live with the consequences? Kids who bust their behinds, work, save, and struggle, are a lot more appreciative of the good things in their lives. **Don't rob your children of the chance to *learn to earn* life's rewards.**

Another common malady related to Affluenza is "Drone" or "Helicopter" parents. Being your child's advocate *is* important. No parent should allow gross humiliation, danger or bullying;

however, a true Momma or Papa Drone is a parent who can be depended on to bail out and make excuses for their child whenever the big, bad outside world steps in with reasonable, natural, real-life consequences for a mistake or lack of effort. Should their child experience failure, Mr. and/or Ms. Drone tend to take on guilt or personal embarrassment for having a less than perfect child. Ralph forgot his homework, cleats, lunch, Chap Stick? No problem, Dad will bring it to him. "That awful teacher *gave* you an *F*? How dare he?" Mamma Drone will go speak to the principal! "You were drunk and fell on the crack in the sidewalk, we'll sue!" "You forgot about the science project that's due tomorrow, Papa will do it for you."

The parents of these unfortunate children are choosing to rob them of the chance to learn valuable life lessons at an age when they could experience consequences on a manageable scale. Might they be more susceptible to negative outside influences without Mama or Papa Drone there to make decisions and fix life for them? Will they look to their "friends" for answers and easy solutions? What can reasonably be expected of these budding adults who have never been held accountable or experienced the consequences of making their own good or bad choices? What does coddling and over-protectiveness teach about personal responsibility, entitlement, being a helpless victim or controlling and manipulative? OK, yes, I'm a bit passionate about this, but avoiding these characteristics is a major goal of *Take the Reins!*

Practice identifying those teachable moments. If it feels like a confrontation is brewing, or your child is about to explode or make a mistake, take a deep breath, inventory your own emotional reactions, ground yourself, and consider if this is an opportunity to teach. **This is mindful parenting.**

Simplify

Simplifying is critical to both healthy brain development and building a connected relationship. You cannot grow either if there isn't unstructured time in your lives for them to blossom. Simplifying your family's life is a terrifically undervalued concept when one considers the impact on our lives of the bombardment of choices available today in acquisitions, information, and electronic entertainment – in everything!

> *"Horses, especially hard working lesson or competition horses need time to just get out and be horses; run, rear, bite, buck, fart, and just be free. It clears the mind and loosens the ropes of stress."*

Many well-intentioned families make life choices that result in over-whelmed parents and children who are entrenched in an over-distracted, over-busy life. I'm not referring here to families enduring truly unavoidable economic, environmental, health or emotional stressors, but to parents who are making life *choices* that result in being stretched too thin.

"I *have* to work 70 hours a week because Rosalia really needs that new SUV and we're working on that 4000 square foot home in the hills."

"Sure, little Otto has room in his schedule today for twenty minutes of park time right after gymnastics and before his Russian class."

"Oh, so sorry, my Adeline's summer is completely filled with camp experiences, so no, she won't be able to spend the afternoon at your house playing Marco Polo in your pool and having a backyard picnic."

When do these families *ever* have time to relax enough to converse and connect? When do these children experience the amazing creativity inspired by being bored or just enjoy a lazy summer afternoon out in nature, so rich with learning and discovery? When do they get a chance to learn to entertain themselves or let their brains delve deeply into some compelling self-directed play, experiment with art, music, or read a book? These unorchestrated activities *should* constitute the majority of childhood.

Simplifying may also mean reexamining expectations of yourself with a "what is more important?" lens. Is it more important that the kids always have their stuff picked up so the house looks like a page from Architectural Digest or that you spend time building a couch cushion hideout with them? Have a clean kitchen or cook with your four year old? Watch that play-off game or get out the sprinklers and make a homemade slip 'n slide? In ten or twenty years which activity will be lovingly remembered? Which will build connection and character?

> *"You can be the maid or you can be emotionally available to your children, but you can't do both."*
> -**Vicki Hoefle**
> ***Duct Tape Parenting***

Take a look at the number of toys your children have readily available. Too many choices are overwhelming and can actually hinder long term ability to make decisions. Rotate toys so there are a limited number of options available at any one time. German kindergartens have even been experimenting, and getting

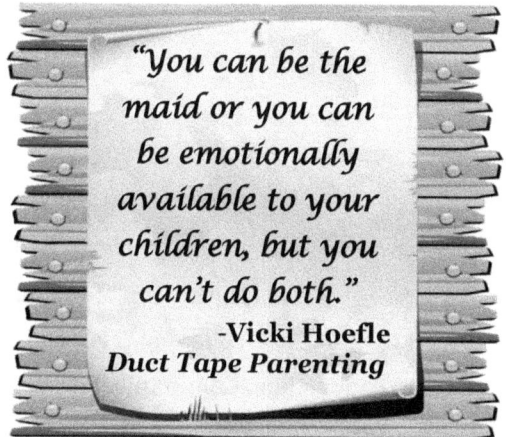

positive results with, weeks of time where no toys are in the classrooms at all. Some of the more recent and successful versions of this idea combine a weekly trip to a nature preserve or the "no toys" weeks are scheduled in the spring or fall when kids can spend more time outside. Teachers observe and facilitate learning, but let the activities be directed by the children. The results are showing increased social skills, creativity, empathy and communication skills. Less definitely can be more.

In over-busy families, when children, frazzled from excess, are whining, spilling, fighting, tantruming, etc., all their over-extended parents have left in their depleted bag of coping skills is to have a come-apart, yell, scream, rant at the world, and often at their child. Three of the many unintentional lessons when this happens are:

♡ The things we are spending our time on are what we value.

♡ This is how one deals with frustration.

♡ This is what *my* life should look like.

The collateral damage is again to the parent-child connection. Communication becomes increasingly abrasive and utilitarian. There isn't time to deeply connect or build a relationship, we're just too busy.

It's a difficult thing to acknowledge that a life-altering transformation is needed, but actually taking the steps necessary to re-examine priorities and simplify for the sake of the children is a monumental task. To further understand the importance of, and how to simplify, I recommend you read the important book *Simplicity Parenting* by Kim John Payne and Lisa M. Ross. They state, "Stress can push the child along on the behavioral spectrum [of diagnosed behavioral issues]. When you simplify a child's life on a number of levels, back they come." **Choose to Simplify**.

"Stress can push the child along on the behavioral spectrum [of diagnosed behavioral issues]. When you simplify a child's life on a number of levels, back they come."
-Kim John Payne and Lisa M. Ross, *Simplicity Parenting*

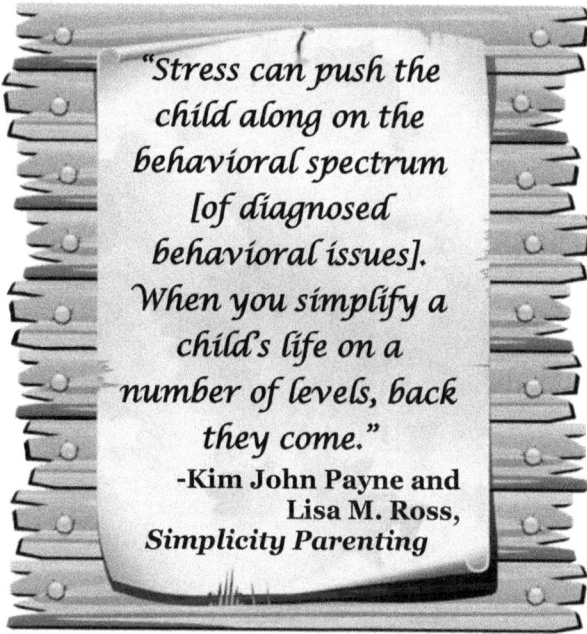

When you utilize teachable moments, hold back on giving, simplify, and let your children learn from their mistakes; when you take the time to explain the logic behind your decisions and stick with them, you teach your child how to make thoughtful decisions. You model how to focus on long term priorities, goals and positive values and how to resist the unnecessary pressures of society, peers and the ever more influential media.

The younger your child is when you adopt an anti-Affluenza, anti-Drone, Simplified frame of mind; the easier it is to live it. Once you've started down the "easy way highway" by giving in, over-protecting, coddling or filling all of their time with stuff, it's extremely hard to change directions because the children's expectations have become a freeway without off ramps! Hat's off to you parents with the forethought and fortitude to make and stick to decisions with long term goals for your children in mind!

Will You Parent as You Were Parented?

There are way too many variables in every child's future to say, "If you'll just live by these five principles, you'll never have any problems with your children." However, every parent has a responsibility to use whatever knowledge is available at the time to be the best, most responsible parent possible. You do *not* want to look back after a life-altering situation and say, "I wish I had done better." You want to look back and know you did the best you could to prepare your child for the inevitable strikes and curve balls that life will throw their way. Implementing change is hard, especially when real life emotions like confusion, anger, grief, fear, frustration and sometimes just life in general, rear their ugly heads. But there are many of us who have proven it can be done.

Horseman and clinician Buck Brannaman was inspired to find another way, at least partly because of serious physical and emotional abuse he experienced in childhood. He cites his difficult, abusive childhood as part of the reason he sought out a different way of being with both horses and his family. Buck could have become an abusive parent himself, but he made a choice to find "a better way of going." He had help along the way from several people including extraordinary foster parents who motivated him to focus on the future and move on from his violent past through love and discipline. Buck said, "Without discipline, it would have been easy to become the kind of man my father was. Kids don't need to be whipped or knocked, any more than I did. They just need to be directed, or re-directed."

Every parent should watch the documentary, "Buck." Especially relevant and poignant is the part where he is dealing with a dangerous stallion that injures his assistant. Buck lets the owner know, in no uncertain terms, that her choices, her lack of knowledge and failure to discipline created this monster that will now need to be put down. If she had recognized that she needed help early on and had been strong, clear and consistent in his training, he may have had at least a chance at a purposeful life. This film was a major inspiration in my decision to apply the wisdom of horsemanship to parenting. It's well worth your time to find it on Netflix or ??.

I didn't experience the degree of abuse that Buck Brannaman did, but it was bad enough; bad enough for me to feel the need to make a choice to do better. At twenty and on track to becoming an art major and possibly an art teacher like my mother; I took my first Child Development class and immediately knew I had to learn more. After earning a degree in the field, I felt at least partially equipped to parent better than I was parented. My two sons would tell you I was not perfect, and if I knew then what I know now, I would have done many things differently. But they were spared the misery of what I experienced as a child and are fine young men.

One of the ways I think we as parents could have done better for our boys is by giving them a better example of how to successfully handle crucial conversations. I know that I took many positive steps toward breaking a negative continuum, but my sons have work to do, too. I can only hope one of the patterns they learned is self-reflection and a desire to improve oneself. If this proves true, I will be grateful to see my sons eventually take the next steps toward being better parents than we were.

Even those lucky folks who's seemingly "Cosby Show" childhoods were filled with wonderful parenting and all those who experienced some variation between ideal and miserable can increase their awareness that they are actually shaping the very development of their children's precious brains. With this weighty knowledge in mind, there is always room for improvement.

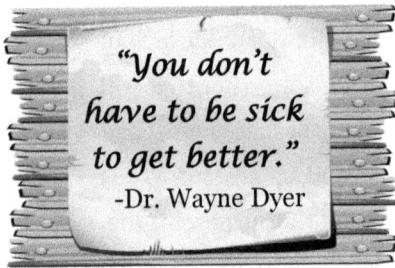

> *"You don't have to be sick to get better."*
> -Dr. Wayne Dyer

One key to motivating your own positive change is to reflect on how you were parented and how it is impacting your parenting choices now. Go back to that important ground work box that asks you to explore how you were parented (Page 59). Discuss it with a friend or partner. Keep the wonderful and take steps to change the not so wonderful.

Reflect on the last time you reacted to a situation less than admirably; when you felt frustrated, incompetent, or reactive and ask yourself where those emotions come from. Unwrap the ugly and the beautiful. Take these feelings out in the open and examine them, uncover the barriers on the path to your improvement. Parenting, like all other life skills, *is* open to growth; it is not written in stone by your history. Free yourself to choose and commit to be the kind of parent you *decide* to be. Create a new and improved continuum.

> *Be who you needed when you were younger.*

The ultimate goal is not just "soft hands" on the reins. The true test of a rider's relationship with her horse is to be able to ride bridleless - with no reins at all. The horse is secure in his abilities, trusts his rider and senses her desires through only her position, weight shifts and intent. He is prepared and willing to go the desired direction and speed without reins controlling him. When your child steps out into the world, you'll want to have built into their psyches positive self-direction and self-control. **You want to be able to let go of the reins with confidence.**

I Got This!

So, you've told yourself, "No problem - I got this!" You've made the decision to blaze a trail toward being a stronger and more loving leader. Well, good! You also know that in order to actually respond with intention in the heat of the moment will take Herculean effort!

For example, Evelyn *knows* that calm and consistent parenting is the best approach to raising kids. Just like she *knows* that reducing sugar, white flour and fat, exercising, and taking everything in moderation, including alcohol, is healthy for her.

Then... she wakes up Monday morning with a pounding headache to find that the baby was the first one to find the juicy hair ball the cat puked up, she's wearing the Cheerios her four year old didn't want for breakfast, and the babysitter just cancelled. She *knows* that the yelling rant that escaped her mouth was wrong and that the giant, warm, crispy apple fritter and strong, very Irish coffee will not help the situation and will likely make it worse, but damn if there isn't perverse bliss in their familiarity and release!

That frontal cortex may know and be absolutely committed to executing the right response, but when push comes to shove, that primitive brain makes it *really* hard to shift into, and act on, "I should." This is why I strongly recommend practice. I implore you – go back and **do the ground work!** Find a partner; maybe have a cocktail if that relaxes you, and role play, write, share. It may feel ridiculous at first, but practice makes, if not perfect, better each time. Your kids deserve your practiced best.

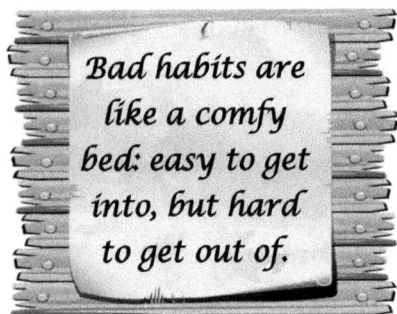

> *Bad habits are like a comfy bed: easy to get into, but hard to get out of.*

Practicing natural horsemanship or becoming a better parent is a process. Start small and set yourself up for success. Give yourself, and your partner Kudos for effort! Changing familiar patterns of parenting is hard and you are to be commended for making the effort. Trust in the knowledge that every little positive change will multiply and spill over into other areas of your life and your children's lives.

Give yourself a break! You won't always do and say just the right thing. If you realize you've said something you shouldn't have or handled a situation badly, good! That's fantastic progress

– you noticed! Review what happened and think through a step by step plan. Next time, how will you specifically respond in a way that teaches something positive? What steps will you need to take to get to where you can act on your plan? The great thing about the concept of the continuum is that it is *a pattern created over time*. One outburst does not mean your child will spend time in juvenile hall.

When you do let your emotions get the better of you and you let go with a tirade, apologize and follow up with at least five connecting actions. Research shows it takes five positives to balance one negative. Positive connecting actions do not mean coming home with a new puppy, a pony or a car! It means taking a deep breath together, sharing a hug, reading a book, acknowledging a try, showing understanding of an emotion; *simple loving connection.*

Keep your apology pure. Do **not** pollute it by using and teaching the relationship destroying *"self-justification"* process: I'm sorry I _____, but **you** should've known better." "If only **you** hadn't _____, then **I** wouldn't have _____," or "Ok, **I** shouldn't have said that, but **you** make me so angry when *you* _____." When you try to resolve the discomfort created by the two contradictory beliefs, "I am a good parent/person," and "I just handled that situation badly," by attempting to justify your actions or words, you negate the apology and teach your children the nasty defensive technique of self-justification. If you want them to use mistakes as learning experiences, it's critical that you model that behavior by owning your mistakes and showing how to learn from them. Simply state, "I was wrong, I'm sorry. I'll do better next time."

> **When you do screw up, apologize... and say "Thank you."**

If you're feeling particularly magnanimous, an additional step is to say "Thank you,"...for being patient with you when you lost your temper, or embarrassed him or her, or whatever your offense was. While an apology teaches the important lesson that it's OK to not be perfect, and to own up to and learn from your mistakes, adding on a "Thank you," takes your interaction to the next level. You are acknowledging the way in which your child responded to the situation and offering a bonus lesson – how to respond when someone else is out of line. She'll learn that preserving and building relationships is more important than being right or winning. She will reap all the benefits of skillfully handling crucial conversations.

TMI

At the risk of sounding just a tad hypocritical, well-meaning analysis and advice from grandparents, friends, books, doctors, teachers, the *always* truthful internet, and random strangers at the grocery store, can cause confusion and even fear. Fear of being too bossy, or being too wimpy, of not doing enough, or doing too much, of saying the wrong thing, of relaxing and actually taking time to connect and enjoy life with your children. Many well-intentioned parents are left understandably hesitant to reach out and pick up the reins.

When you have thought carefully about yourself and your child and the non-negotiable principles that you will embrace as the core of your parenting approach, you can then open yourself up to new ideas, research, strategies and interpretations. You can explore how and if new information fits into those principles by doing some ground work. Discuss, experiment, practice with a partner. Only then should you *confidently* apply what rings true to your actual parenting interactions. Include your child in the process of change with a, "Let's figure this out together as a family," approach. Hopefully you will use the principles you've learned here as a guide to decide if and how, to confidently incorporate new information.

Be prepared to discipline. Observe, listen, think, plan ahead, and challenge yourself to grasp those teachable moments and respond with long term learning in mind. Confident and consistent leadership is the key to raising confident, responsible and resilient children. From the vantage point of an elder, though it may not seem like it now, their childhood passes unimaginably fast. You'll want to know when they're grown, that you did the best you could. You don't get do-overs.

Happy parenting trails to you,

Kris & Hannah

References

Some great web reads - worth a copy 'n paste into your browser.

http://www.parentinghorsesense.com

http://www.theinterpretedrock.com/2012/02/natural-horsemanship-and-parenting.html

http://www.nytimes.com/2014/10/17/us/quality-of-words-not-quantity-is-crucial-to-language-skills-study-finds.html?_r=1

http://www.cnn.com/2011/09/06/living/teachers-want-to-tell-parents/index.html?c&page=3

http://www.positiveparentingsolutions.com/parenting/notice-good-children

http://www.dropyourreins.com/danielle-herb-drop-your-reins-horse-program-for-add-adhd-and-autistic-kids/

http://findingjoy.net/20-things-not-to-regret-doing-with-kids/

http://centerforparentingeducation.org/library-of-articles/responsibility-and-chores/part-i-Dorcasefits-of-chores/

http://www.huffingtonpost.com/rachel-macy-stafford/the-important-thing-about-yelling_b_4484027.html?utm_hp_ref=fb&src=sp&comm_ref=false

http://www.huffingtonpost.com/kate-bartolotta/10-things-i-want-to-tell-my-kids-before-theyre-too-cool-to-

TAKE THE REINS!

listen_b_Five142810.html?fb_action_ids=6Five6483FiveFive1101Five1Five&fb_action_types=og.likes

http://www.huffingtonpost.com/liz-evans/2Five-ways-to-ask-your-kids-so-how-was-school-today-without-asking-them-so-how-was-school-todaybFive738338.html

http://www.cnn.com/2014/07/23/health/effects-spanking-brain/

http://www.positiveparentingsolutions.com/parenting/unhelpful-things-parents-say

http://community.today.com/parentingteam/post/how-a-bucket-list-eliminated-my-mom-guilt?cid=eml_tpt_20170528

http://www.drlaura.com/b/What-Teens-Should-Pay-For/-21673744984732631.html?utm_campaign=090Five14Teens-Pay&utm_medium=blog&utm_source=facebook&utm_content=09.0Five.14&utm_term=link

On Consistency - http://www.horsechannel.com/horse-news/2014/09/23-is-your-horse-unsafe.aspx

Anita Renfro – Momisms
https://www.youtube.com/watch?v=YYukEAmoMCQ

A commercial I think everyone should hear & see, especially parents of girls. (Also any commercial First 5 California puts out)
http://www.wimp.com/hearspretty/

Dr. Wendy McCord, http://www.wendymccord.com/ (Book and Video available)

The Horse Whisperers:

Anita Markiewcz: http://kisshorses.com/
Buck Brannaman: http://brannaman.com/
Julie Goodnight: http://juliegoodnight.com/
Kathleen Lindley Beckham: http://www.kathleenlindley.com/
Mark Rashid: markrashid.com
Pat Parelli: http://www.parelli.com/
Ray Hunt: http://www.rayhunt.com/
Richard Winters: http://www.wintersranch.com/
Tom Dorrance: http://tomdorrance.com/

Some great reads:

Bronson, Po and Merryman, Ashley. *NurtureShock: New Thinking About Children.* New York, Hatchette Book Group, 2009

Bryson, Tina, and Siegel, Daniel. *The Whole-Brain Child: Twelve Revolutionary Strategies to Nurture Your Child's Developing Mind.* New York, Bantam Books 2012 York, Ballantine Books, 2008

Druckerman, Pamela, *Bringing Up Bébé, One American Mother Discovers the Wisdom of French Parenting,* The Penguin Press 2014

Dweck, Carol S. Phd., *Mindset, The New Psychology of Success.* New York, Balantine Books 2006, 2016

Faber, Adele and Mazlish, Elaine. *How to Talk so Kids Will Listen & Listen so Kids Will Talk,* New York, Avon Books 1980

Hoefle, Vicki, *Duct Tape Parenting: A Less is More Approach to Raising Respectful, Responsible, & Resilient Kids.* Brookline, MA, Bibliomotion, Inc., 2012

McCord, Wendy, PhD, LMFCT: Video available on website *Between Humans & Horses: Eight Parenting Lessons from the Horse's Mouth*, also, coming soon, a new edition of *Earthbabies*

Kurcinka, Mary Sheedy. *Kids, Parents and Power Struggles*. New York, HarperCollins 2000

Pantley, Elizabeth. *Kid Cooperation: How to Stop Yelling, Nagging, and Pleading and Get Kids to Cooperate*. Oakland, CA, New Harbinger Publications, Inc. 1996

Patterson, Kerry, Grenny, Alfred, McMillan, Rufus, Switzler, Al. *Crucial Conversations: Tools for Talking When the Stakes are High*, McGraw-Hill, New York 2012

Payne, Kim John and Ross, Lisa M. *Simplicity Parenting*: *Using the Extraordinary Power of Less to Raise Calmer, Happier, and More Secure Kids*. New York, Ballantine Books 2010

Rashid, Mark – Every book by this author.

Sax, Leonard, MD, PhD, *The Collapse of Parenting; How We Hurt Our Kids When We Treat Them like Grown-Ups*, Basic Books 2015

Smalley, Sue and Winston Diana, *Fully Present, the Science, Art and Practice of Mindfulness*, Da Capo Press 2010

Tomasky, Tracy, *The Conscious And Courageous Leader: Developing Your Authentic Voice To Lead And Inspire*, Chrysalis Coaching Press 2016

Tough, Paul, *How Children Succeed: Grit, Curiosity, and the Hidden Power of Character*, Houghton Mifflin Harcourt 2012